UNLOCKING THE

A Commentary on
1 & 2 THESSALONIANS

David Pawson

Anchor Recordings

First published in Great Britain in 2015 by
Anchor Recordings Ltd
72 The Street, Kennington, Ashford TN24 9HS

**For more of David Pawson's teaching,
including DVDs and CDs, go to
www.davidpawson.com**

**FOR FREE DOWNLOADS
www.davidpawson.org**

**For further information, email
info@davidpawsonministry.org**

ISBN 978-1-909886-73-5

Printed by Lightning Source

A Commentary on
1 & 2 THESSALONIANS

Contents

COVER ILLUSTRATION

The illustration on the front cover represents a real photograph which had been taken during a storm in the mid 1980s and was subsequently given to David Pawson.

An Australian lady was travelling to New Zealand from Australia when the flight entered a violent electrical storm, tossing the plane all over the sky. Many passengers were panicking and screaming, but she and the lady next to her were Christians, so the two of them prayed and asked the Lord to bring them through, to calm the storm as he did at Galilee. Immediately, the plane came through into clear air. Looking out of the window she tried to take a picture of the lightning.

It was not until she landed in New Zealand, and was able to take the film to be developed that she realised what images she had captured. The owner of the shop that developed the film asked, "Where did you take this picture?" She told him the story before he gave her the photograph, so she had not seen the image until that moment. You can see an outline that looks like the image of Christ there in the clouds.

This book is based on a series of talks. Originating as it does from the spoken word, its style will be found by many readers to be somewhat different from my usual written style. It is hoped that this will not detract from the substance of the biblical teaching found here.

As always, I ask the reader to compare everything I say or write with what is written in the Bible and, if at any point a conflict is found, always to rely upon the clear teaching of scripture.

David Pawson

1

Read 1 Thessalonians 1

A. PRAYER (2–3)
1. Faith that works
2. Love that labours
3. Hope that endures

B. PREDESTINATION (4)
1. Divine sovereignty
2. Human responsibility

C. PREACHING (5a)
1. Word of gospel
2. Power of Spirit

D. PRACTICE (5b–10)
1. Imitation – rejoicing
    a. Apostles
    b. Lord
2. Model – repenting
    a. Turn from past
    b. Serve in present
    c. Wait for future

In our culture and civilization, we tend to worship success. We speak about being successful in our examinations, successful in our careers. If you hear someone say "he's been a successful man" it is intriguing to know what they mean. Now there is nothing wrong or inherently sinful with being successful. But the word of caution I want to give straightaway is that what we think is success may not be what God counts as success. For example, someone who makes a lot of money and builds up a big business and has great plans for his retirement is not in the eyes of the Lord a successful man, he is a fool, because everything he has he will leave behind. He could leave it behind any night when he goes to bed.

Some years ago I saw a series of articles about successful churches – the very title makes me shudder. But it is intriguing to analyse why certain churches have such a reputation. Alas, people use this word "successful" of big congregations or big collections or a multiplicity of activities and busyness. That may be very far from what God counts as a successful church. The thought that came to me most clearly as I read 1 Thessalonians 1 is that right there in that chapter is the answer to the question "What is a successful church?"

Before we jump right in to the answer, let me just say a little by way of introduction to this letter, about the place Thessalonica and the Christians there. I am intrigued with the address "To the church of the Thessalonians in God". If you lived (as we did) in Guildford, it is as though Paul wrote a letter and addressed it to "the church of the Guildfordians in God". We tend to think the opposite way around, which shows how far we have come from New Testament thinking. We might say "the church of God in Guildford". Where do you really live? What is your real address? Our real address then would have been the church of Guildford living in God.

Let us look at Thessalonica. Greece has left its mark on our educational system in this country, but once it was the centre of a vast empire. A young man called Alexander set out from Greece to conquer the world. By the age of thirty-three he had done it and was dead. That young man was found weeping in his tent because there were no more worlds to conquer. He had gone as far as Egypt, as far as India, and he had conquered everything before him. His dream was one united world with Greek architecture and Greek language. He saw himself as the world's saviour, uniting the world in Greek culture. Those were the great days of Greece, but they did not last. They lasted no longer than the young man. After he died, his empire broke up and Greece shrank back from an empire to being just one country, as Britain has shrunk from being an empire to just a little country.

Greece split into two parts: Macedonia in the north and Achaia in the south. In the north, Macedonia, Alexander's home country, there were towns named after his family. There was Philippi named after his father, Philip, and there was Thessalonica, named after his sister. It is that town we are talking about now. It probably had a hundred and fifty to two hundred thousand people in it even then. It sat astride the main road of the world – the road that went from Rome to India, the main way from east to west. The capital of Macedonia, Thessalonica was a town governed by a democratically elected assembly. This was the first time that Christianity had come into a democracy. That is an intriguing point because it comes out in the letter in certain things that Paul says.

Now let us look at Paul, who was the first missionary to come with the gospel of Christ to the capital of Macedonia, astride the east-west road. What happened in this city would happen right along that road. If you could establish your business or your firm in Thessalonica, you would soon have branches everywhere. It was a key place. If the gospel could take root here, it would travel everywhere. Paul, when he brought the gospel to Europe (and it was God who told him to come) preached in Philippi, the first big town he reached. But then you notice in Acts 17 that he went past town after town until he came to Thessalonica before he preached again. The reason was very simple: this was the key town. If he could plant a church here, then the whole of Macedonia – indeed the whole of Greece – could be changed. In a sense, Paul was coming in the reverse direction to Alexander the Great, to conquer for Christ. In the name of another young man who died at the age of thirty-three, but who rose again from the dead, Paul was going to reverse the process of history.

Alexander the Great had left one vitally important thing behind him wherever he had gone throughout the then known world. It is true that he left traces of the Greek culture like Corinthian pillars and the architecture you can see still in the main buildings in London – the Royal Exchange and the Bank of England – and you can see traces of Greek architecture the world over. But the main thing Alexander left behind him was the Greek language.

Everywhere he had gone, people learned Greek as a second language. The result was that when Paul came to conquer for Christ with the gospel, with no weapons but words, he could use the language that Alexander had planted everywhere three hundred years earlier. It was that language that caused the gospel to sweep through the Roman Empire. The Romans now occupied it and the Greeks were "has beens", but even the Romans still learned Greek as a second language. It was the one language you could use everywhere in the world.

Paul came in the name of Jesus, using the Greek language, and every bit of the New Testament was written in the language of Alexander. God, I believe, overruled Alexander the Great's conquests so that he left the language behind in which the gospel could be preached and in which another conqueror, who died at thirty-three, could claim the world for himself. That one would succeed and his name was Jesus Christ. So Paul came in the reverse direction and retraced Alexander's footsteps back to Alexander's home country, Macedonia, back to Philippi—named after Alexander's father, back to Thessalonica—named after his sister. There Paul planted churches and paid for it by going to prison, by being flogged, by being turned out of town – what a man!

I remember reading a very amusing little article once in a Christian magazine. It was a magazine in which somebody imagined a church meeting looking for a new pastor. They were discussing someone who had been recommended to them by name – Saul, the Reverend Saul. They were discussing whether he would be a suitable pastor. One member got up in the meeting and said, "Well, I think we ought to know that he has never stayed too long in any place, sometimes only a few weeks. I gather the longest was about three years. Don't we want somebody to stay a little longer than that?"

Then somebody else got up and said, "I have heard he has been in trouble with the police in one or two places." Somebody else says, "Yes, I've heard that, and he was actually in prison. Do we want a pastor who has been in prison?"

Someone else added, "Well you know, he's not very impressive in personal appearance. In fact, he's got something funny with his eyes you know. He doesn't look very good; we've got to think of our image in town."

You can imagine them discussing this minister. Then, to cap it all, somebody gets up and says, "On top of all that we've said, you know, he speaks in tongues."

Immediately you can sense the reaction. The church meeting says, "Oh well, I think we had better look somewhere else."

Is it not lovely that God uses the very people that man would not choose? So often, God can choose someone to conquer the world who nobody would ever dream of choosing as a leader. Yet this little Jew, Paul, came. The only description we have of him is of a bald head, bushy eyebrows meeting in the middle, bow legs, and not a very impressive appearance. But this little man was coming to conquer more than Alexander the Great ever conquered; he came in the name and the power of Jesus, not by himself.

Paul was not one of those leaders who has to be a loner. Too much Christian work has suffered from individualists who work on their own. Paul knew that it is God's wish that there be teamwork, so he always had a companion; in this case he had Silas and, later, Timothy. They went to prison together, they preached together, but there was always a team. Our Lord sent people out two by two. That is the very minimum you need to establish a good Christian work, better still if you have a team with more.

So Paul and Silas came to Philippi and found themselves in the stocks at midnight in prison, singing hymns. Thrown out the next day, escorted to the border, they went out with some dignity. Paul said to the civic authorities, "You put us in prison wrongly; you can escort us out." Being shown to the city borders gave Paul a chance to talk to them and witness to them on the way. Then they came to Thessalonica, preached, got into trouble, and very soon had to flee the city.

I do not know if it was just three weeks, as some scholars say, or a month or two, but one thing is certain: within the short time they were in Thessalonica they had the most successful mission they had ever had anywhere. Whenever Paul said his prayers after that, he thanked God for what was happening in Thessalonica. He says that at the beginning of the letter. It was a success. There is nothing wrong with the right sort of success.

Isn't it thrilling when you are praying for someone or something to be able to recall the mighty acts of God and what God can do in a place? Let me give glory to God for something that happened when I was in the Methodist ministry, in Lancashire. The Methodist conference sent me to an address: Eliza Street, Ramsbottom, and you can't get more Lancashire than that. I remember it as a tough situation. For eighteen months we laboured and did not see much fruit. We left the place and I went to be pastor at Chalfont St. Peter straight from there in 1961. But left behind was one young man called Alan who had come to the Lord. He was in his early twenties. He made a living repairing electric razors and at first Alan, who was to be God's man, just worked quietly among the young people. He learned to play football well so that he could start a football team. Soon, he had sixty boys meeting in a crusader class. He went on steadily and gradually the older people came to respect him. He prayed and worked. The church building was one of those big Lancashire chapels built on the principle of pulling down your barns and building greater. A great stone building, it could probably have held about eight or nine hundred people. It was a great empty barn of a place with people looking lost in it.

He rang me up and was bubbling over. He said, "It's our centenary. You know what – the Baptists and Methodists have now joined up and we are all together and one. So now we have got two ministers – a Baptist and a Methodist. The Methodist minister is preaching the gospel now and we're celebrating our centenary; it's a mini revival." He began to list names of those I had known and tried to get through to and tried to preach to, and who had seemed as hard as the

1 & 2 THESSALONIANS

stone walls. Naming them, he said, "So and so has come to the Lord and is radiant, and so and so has come to the Lord. Our church was packed this morning; we're looking forward to tonight. It's hit the place." Thrilling. So one could pray for them and thank God that he really has worked. In a situation that one despaired of that number of years ago, God sent revival. I know that the secret behind what has happened there in the last year or two will be the same secret that we are going to find in 1 Thessalonians 1. What is the secret of success? What makes a successful church? What is a successful church? I will tell you straightaway and put you out of your suspense and give you the answer. It is not a church with a lot of people in it; it is not a church with a lot of money in it; it is not a church with a lot of meetings in it; nor is it a church with a lot of busy people in it. It is a church with a lot of faith and a lot of hope and a lot of love in it – that is a successful church. It may be small or large. It may have a lovely building or meet in a tin shed. It is a community that has the marks of God's family. So Paul says, "When I pray for you constantly, I give thanks to God." For what? For your faith, your love, and your hope. Notice the order.

Incidentally, he usually puts them this way around because faith is primarily related to what is past and has happened. Love is primarily related to the present and what is happening now, and hope is related to the future. So he gives thanks to God for their faith, love and hope. That is how God measures a church.

I want you to notice that it is not only faith, hope and love. Paul adds a word to each which turns them into very active things. He says: what I thank God for is a faith that acts, and a love that labours and a hope that holds on. You see faith that does not act is not faith at all. Your faith is not what you recite or even what you sing; it is what you depend upon. There was a prayer meeting in the north of England where some farmers met to pray for rain in a time of drought. The crops were failing and they needed rain. But one little girl turned up at the meeting with an umbrella. Paul says, "I thank God that you have a faith that acts". That is the kind of faith that you can measure a church by. Is a church adventurous? Is a church constantly stretching beyond its own resources? Is it constantly tackling problems that are too big for it? Has it got its sights beyond its own reach? Or is it just doing things in the flesh? Is it a faith that acts? Is it a faith that really does works?

Secondly, is it a love that labours? There is an idea around that love is primarily how you *feel*. It is not – it is *what you do about how you feel*. Jesus taught this – it is whether you help the man who has fallen among thieves.

Of course, you do need to feel affection and God can give you that but it is still what you do about it that matters. I confess publicly that one day I sinned against my wife: I came downstairs in the morning and there was a card waiting for me – a wedding anniversary congratulation. Now she knows I love her, but I think she would have been happier if I had done something about it. Paul says: I thank God for a love that labours – a love that really works at it, a love that toils until it is tired. I thank God for a hope that hangs on. Too many hopes in the world don't hang on, they get dashed. Of course they do, for a very simple reason. Paul says, "I thank God for your faith, your love, and your hope in the Lord Jesus Christ." Outside of him, none of those three things really can do the job. There is plenty of faith in the world, but it is not faith in the Lord Jesus. There is plenty of hope in the world, but it is not hope in him. There is plenty of love in the world, but unless it is love in him you cannot build up the community that God wants. So there is a successful church for you – a church in which there is lots of faith that is acting and lots of love that is caring and lots of hope that is holding on.

How do you get there? How do you get a successful church? In the rest of chapter one, Paul gives the secret very simply. There are three steps to a successful church: predestination; preaching; practice. Were you surprised when I began with predestination? That is where Paul began.

Paul says, "We know that you were chosen of God, beloved brethren." I do not care what you think about predestination, to the Christian it is a most precious truth. Some people make predestination into an arbitrary thing as if God just picks people out with a pin, but that is not predestination. Some people make predestination a harsh thing and make out that God is just choosing a few favourites and damning the rest. Some people make predestination into an uncertain thing so that you can never be quite sure who is chosen. All those ideas are wrong.

Paul says, "We know you are chosen." You can be certain of predestination. We *know*. What it means is this: God does not do anything unless he decides to do it. A successful church does not begin with the decision of man, but a decision of God. It is his initiative. Wherever you have a successful church, you mistakenly try to attribute that to some human agency but it is God who has chosen. It is God who has decided to work. It is God who took the initiative and he did it out of sheer love. He chose to work out of love. God's choice is not arbitrary. We know why he chooses and we know how he chooses. The Bible tells us. God loves to choose nobodies. So if you want to see God work, you get in among a lot of nobodies. God is more likely to choose that situation in which to work than where there are a lot of clever people who do not trust him. We know how God chooses and the first step is predestination.

When Paul came to Thessalonica, he came because God

chose Thessalonica as the next centre of preaching. When Paul preached, things began to happen. So Paul says, "We know that God has chosen you because of what happened when we preached." The simple fact is that I can preach my heart out from a pulpit and some of the people will go away the same people as they came and others will have been touched by God. It will be God who took the initiative, not me. I just cannot deny that fact that it is God's choice.

There are twenty-seven areas in the world today where there is revival. Why is it happening in twenty-seven areas? The answer is that God has chosen. Outside those twenty-seven areas there are localities where God has chosen to work. It is his choice; it is he who sets the whole ball rolling – "There will be a church for my name in that area." Predestination is step number one and it is always God's initiative. Therefore, that is where the praise and glory ought to be. The tragedy is that we look at churches as we look at businesses, when we say that it must be due to the businessman, and it is not. It is because God in his mercy and grace chose to plant a church in a particular place.

Now the second step is *preaching*. God has still chosen this as the main means of establishing a church. One of the things that worries me today among my fellow ministers, is the drop in morale about preaching and ministers losing confidence in preaching, feeling that it must be replaced with anything. But it is not gimmicks and it is not just trying to keep a thing up, and it is not a human building up. I believe that preaching is still the main thing that God uses to build a church up. Though we can use all the other things, and we can use music, dance, art, dialogue and theatre – anything I believe can be sanctified to the Lord if it is wholesome in itself. Nevertheless, I believe it is through the preaching of the gospel basically – but a certain kind of preaching. There must be thousands of sermons being preached at this moment. Why does God build a church in one place and not in another? Paul is teaching us that it has to be a certain kind of preaching.

Real preaching that leads to a successful church must have three marks. First, it must be the preaching of the gospel – not of human opinions, not of the latest reading the man has done in his study, not the latest news headlines, but the gospel, the Word of God. It never goes out of date and it never ceases to be relevant. You can have preaching that is not the preaching of the gospel, and where it is not, God will not build a successful church. But the other two marks are equally necessary. You can hear someone preach and the sermon is as sound as a bell theologically but the people are fast asleep. Why? Two other dimensions are missing.

The second dimension of true preaching is the power of the Spirit. That is something that cannot be turned on. A man may preach, he may get excited, he may wave his arms around, he may try to replace the power of the Spirit with his own energy and effort, but it is God who witnesses to his gospel. When the power of the Spirit is changing lives – in other words, when something is happening in the pew as well as in the pulpit – a church will be built up. If nothing is happening in the pew, it doesn't matter how much is happening in the pulpit, the church is not built. The power of the Spirit does that.

Paul says, "We came to you with the word of the gospel and in the power of the Spirit and with full conviction." That is when the Spirit is working as well as the preacher. When people can see that lives are being touched and changed, and when they can see that the gospel works and that it does deliver people from fears and sins and guilt and that it really works, when they can see the Spirit moving, that kind of preaching will build up a church.

The third dimension – and this is even more personal to

those of us who are preachers – is the life of the preacher. In particular, it is how dedicated he is to the gospel he preaches, whether he is prepared to toil and work hard for it, whether he is prepared to suffer for it, whether it really means everything to him, or whether it is a professional job twice a Sunday and that is all. The public are not fools and they say, "How much does this really mean to the man who's preaching?" Paul says, "You know what kind of men we prove to be among you," and that is the third dimension. Where those three dimensions are present, I will guarantee you that God will choose to build a successful church and he will use that kind of preaching.

Now we will turn away from the preachers to the pew. The third step is *practice*. You can have all the preaching you like in the pulpit, but unless what is preached is also practised by those who hear, nothing will happen. At this point I want to use the word "imitation". Paul says, "You became imitators of us and of the Lord." Most things we learn in life we learn by imitation. Watch your little girl with a doll, and she is holding the doll in her arm and she is dressing the doll and washing it. Where did she learn to do that? She has learned by imitating her mother with the baby. Watch that boy—he is imagining he is driving a car and he is in his pedal car. How did he learn to do this? By imitation.

There is learning a sport—I remember trying to learn badminton. Someone explained what to do: "Hold your racket like this and bend your wrists like this. Do it like this." I was trying to imitate, and I was learning by imitation. So Paul teaches that this is the way to practise what is being preached – imitate someone who is practising it. There is nothing wrong with imitation as long as you are imitating the right things. Don't imitate the outside of a Christian life – don't just open your mouth and sing hymns, that produces imitation Christians, but imitate the faith, the hope and the love of others. Imitate their trust in God. Do the same thing as they are doing towards the Lord and see what happens. Pray as they pray and see what happens. Imitation is the first step. Paul says, "You imitated us and, therefore, you became an example to everybody else." I will tell you this: a successful church needs no publicity. "Word went out from Thessalonica," says Paul, "like a clap of thunder or like the peal of a trumpet through the whole of Macedonia, through the whole of Achaia." The whole of Greece heard about this church and it was talked about. Why? Because people were practising what was preached.

A preacher may be able to draw an audience, but a successful church is one where the practice of the members is talked about. "So that not only," says Paul, "do you talk about the Lord, but others talk about you too." It is that double testimony which puts a church on the map and which makes people want to say, "I must go and find out. God is among them; something's happening. I want to go and see." You don't need to advertise when a house is on fire. People want to see and they appear from nowhere and want to come and look.

How do you practise? What does Paul mean by practising? I finish with this. Three verbs he uses: people who *turn*, people who *serve*, and people who *wait*. I want to ask you: is it true of you that you are someone who has turned, who is serving, and who is waiting? If so, then faith, hope, and love will appear in your fellowship. If you just listen to sermons and you do not do any of those three things, then frankly the report will not go out that God is present, and a church will not be a success in God's eyes. So let us look at these three verbs Paul uses.

When he came to Thessalonica he said, "You turned from idols to God and you are serving God, the true and living God. You are waiting for Jesus to come back." These are the three first simple steps that someone takes towards faith, hope and love. The moment that he turns to God, he has begun faith. The moment that he begins to serve the true and living God he has begun to love. The moment he begins to wait for Jesus' coming, he has begun to hope, and that is how they begin. We have almost come full circle, back to the first verse – turn.

I meet many people who think that they can become Christians by going right on in the same direction, which they have already travelled, only they simply ask Jesus to accompany them. Do not believe it! The only way to become a Christian is to turn from idols to God. It involves a turn because you were heading in the wrong direction. The reason why most people cannot see God is because they have got their backs to him. The only way they will begin is to turn from idols. Somebody may say, "Well, I don't bow down to a lump of wood or stone." Don't you? What has first place in your life? What is the one thing or person that you say, "You could take everything else away, but don't take that?" What are you trusting to see you through the problems that lie ahead? What is your idol?

I know some parents who idolise their children; some men idolise their latest car. Some just idolise themselves, and that is the worst idol of all to have. But whatever is first in your affections, your ambitions, your loyalties; whatever is top is your idol, whatever it may be. Have you ever asked yourself, "What did I turn away from to become a Christian?" If the answer is "nothing", then I really wonder whether you became a Christian. There is a turn involved, not just away from something but to God.

Do you know what idols were in the ancient world? They were lumps of wood or stone that were there to help people to worship. Sometimes our idol may even be something that helps us to worship. It may be a church building; it may be a particular minister. It may be a form of worship; it may be a particular hymn book. Even these things can become idols. Even the Bible can become an idol. We turn from all this and we turn to God. Then all the other things take their rightful place.

Let me give you an illustration. There was a lady whose idol was babies. Can you imagine that? She was single, but she worshipped babies. Her job was to look after babies; she was a nanny, a nurse. She went to families that could afford it and she looked after their babies. She says she worshipped babies. Now she claimed to believe in God, but the first love of her life was babies. I remember her giving her testimony in church about how the Lord had to get her away from babies totally, to bring her to himself. She turned away from the babies and then, robbed of her idols, she turned to the living God and she found him. Years later, God put her in charge of a Salvation Army orphanage and gave her back more babies then she had ever had before. But now, they took second place.

Turn. A successful church begins when people turn from anything or anyone who is number one in their life and turn to God as number one and say, "From now on, it's you first." To serve the living God. You were not saved to enjoy yourself. You were saved to serve and service is the very essence of the Christian life. We are here not just to enjoy ourselves and to have a happy time, we are here to serve the true and living God. A successful church will be made up of those who have turned to God and are now serving God. They do not ask, "What is the minimum that I can do for him?" They do not immediately get defensive if the minister or someone calls because, "Oh, what's he going to ask me to do now?" They say, "I want to serve God with everything I've got. My joy is his service; his service is perfect freedom. I want to go on working all my life; I never want to retire from this service. I want to use my whole life to serve him."

Finally, there are those who *wait*. Christians are people who are waiting. The tragedy is that you can go into churches where you never hear the Lord's Second Coming mentioned. There could be people there who are not thrilled to look forward to that event. We are waiting. "Even so, come Lord Jesus."

A Christian is someone who not only *has turned* and *is serving*, but also i*s waiting*. What for? Waiting for the second visit of the Son of God to this planet. That is the dimension of hope that is there in the kind of church that is constantly thinking of our Lord's Second Coming – there you find hope that holds on and is never disappointed. Did you turn? Are you serving? Are you waiting? Then you will be part of a successful church where there is a faith that acts, a love that cares and a hope that endures.

Speak to the Lord and respond and reply to him now. He is asking you, "Have you turned to me from that which you hold most dear?" If you know you did turn to him, he is saying, "Are you serving me as you should?" If you are serving him as you should, he is asking you, "Are you waiting for me? Are you really looking forward to leaving your home and your present situation and really coming to be with me, or are you getting too settled down where you are? Are you waiting?"

Answer the Lord in your own words, in your own way, and speak to him in your heart.

2

Read 1 Thessalonians 2:1–16

PAST RELATIONS

1. What they were not (1–6)
    a. Mixed motives
    b. Deceitful desires

2. What they were (7–16)
    a. Mother
    b. Father
    c. Brothers

I am often asked if people today can believe in a personal devil. That belief requires no faith on my part, it is a matter of fact – plain everyday experience. I have discovered that as soon as you believe in a personal God you come right smack up against a personal devil. I am very sympathetic towards the Scotland Yard inspector who pointed out that sometimes in London there is an outbreak of petty crime. When they capture the criminals and question them, they discover that many of them do not have the intelligence to have thought out the crimes they committed. The police then know that there is a new king of the underworld, and they open a file, "Mr. X" and gradually, from what he does to the people in his control, they build up a picture of his character and fill out the details until they know exactly the kind of man they are looking for. Similarly, I have never met the devil face-to-face but I am sure that he exists.

One of the things I know about the devil is this: he hates successful evangelism. He hates successful churches and he hates any situation in which the Word of God is setting people free, and he will do anything within his power to stop that work going on. Fortunately, we are not in ignorance about how he sets about this. We are not ignorant of his devices, we know what we are up against and we know how he will set about undoing the work of the gospel of our Lord Jesus Christ.

There are three devices in particular I want to mention. The first is that, if he possibly can, he will attack the message that is being preached. If he can, he will stop people preaching the Bible, preaching a straightforward gospel. You see, it is an old, old story – two thousand years old. Although we need to change the package, the content does not change. We need to change the language and the illustrations but the gospel itself never changes.

In an age that seeks novelty, when people want something

fresh they have not heard before, there is an awful temptation on the preacher to try and bring novelty to the pulpit. The devil loves novelty, anything that is supposed to be modern and fashionable. So he gets people to change the old story into something new, and the result is that conversions cease, people are not set free, and lives are not changed. I believe that one of the greatest victories the devil has had in England is to persuade preacher after preacher to try to be modern and to regard the old-fashioned gospel as too out-of-date.

If the devil does not succeed in getting a preacher off the old message, then the next thing he will do is attack the messenger. If he cannot succeed in that, he will then attack the hearers to try to stop them hearing the message. The devil is attacking the gospel at every one of these points.

The word "Satan" means slanderer, liar, and he is the father of all lies. When we read between the lines of 1 Thessalonians 2, we find that they were saying horrible things about Paul in Thessalonica. You notice they were saying them after he had gone. The devil does not usually talk to a person's face, he always says things in such a way that the rumour has spread before it gets to the man himself. Paul realised what was being said and if we read between the lines we can see what kind of horrible slander was being put in the minds of that church about the very man who had founded the church, who had brought them the gospel and set them free.

First of all, they were saying he was a bungler and that wherever he went he left a bigger mess than he found and that he was ineffective as a servant of the Lord, and that when he had gone, you would have far more problems than when he came. They were also saying that he was a coward and had run away from the situation. We know of course from the Bible that he had left the situation because he did not want to bring the believers into trouble.

They said all kinds of other horrible things about him – probably because he was single and they were told that many of the leading women came; they said he was a womaniser. They said he was a confidence trickster and that he came full of guile. They said he was a religious maniac, they said he was an exploiter, an opportunist, and that he was only in it for the cash; they saw that collections were taken in the meetings. They said he was a lazy man and that he was only in preaching because he could not do a day's work. They said he was a dictator, probably because he was a very determined character.

They were saying all these things and many more and if you read between the lines, it is a pretty horrible list. Funnily enough, you will find contrary things being said about a messenger of God, and if you listen to all of them as in this case you can cancel most of them out with each other. He could not be a religious maniac and a confidence trickster at the same time! Read 1 Thessalonians 2 carefully and you find that there were all kinds of horrible things. And had they been able to prove them, then the devil would have won the battle and the gospel would have stopped its work in Thessalonica.

How the devil operates is to take true facts, otherwise people would not listen, and then he twists them, building a false construction on those true facts. It is sad but true that when we criticise one another, we are in fact revealing ourselves. When we go on criticising we are revealing that we judge others by ourselves. When the devil says these kinds of things, he is simply revealing what he is like. If the devil were an ordained minister, as he preached the gospel he would be in it for what he could get out of it. And he would be doing those things of which he accused Paul through those who talked. The devil simply is this kind of person and assumes that everybody else is like him. Of course, the tragedy is that until we are redeemed by Christ we are just like him – we are of our father, the devil, until Christ has put us right. A man can preach the gospel from many different motives. That is the tragedy of it and this passage makes us all examine our own hearts, whether you preach to a thousand or one does not matter, these motives apply. "What's in it for you?" says the devil, revealing his own heart.

In 1 Thessalonians 2, Paul stands in the dock and defends himself, and he calls witnesses into the court to answer these charges. He calls two witnesses to the witness box – as God is my witness and as you are my witness, Thessalonians. He conducts his own case with brilliant strategy. Some of the charges he denies, some of them he argues about, but all of them he faces. As we go through this chapter we shall find that Paul was able to appeal to one thing after another to which we must be able to appeal.

First, in v. 1, to his effectiveness. He is not a bungler. He says, "You know, you are my witness; you know that when I came to Thessalonica it was not to no effect. I'm not a bungler; I knew what I was doing. I haven't messed up the situation; I've left behind me a strong church full of faith, hope, and love." That's not a bungler's work; a bungler can't do that.

There was a man of God called Billy Richards, a Pentecostal pastor in Slough. Many years ago he started a work of God in a chicken hut with a leaking roof. They had six buckets on the floor to catch the rain that first service. Six or seven men gathered in that little hut. But by the time he was taken to glory, in that church in Slough, you would find seven or eight hundred people there worshipping God. They had sixteen daughter groups scattered around Slough and its environment. They had a correspondence course for some enquirers, and some 2,000 people learning how to be Christians. They had 40 missionaries working overseas. That is not the work of a bungler, it is the work of a man who knows what he is doing, a man who is effective. Wherever Paul went, he left an effective church behind and the charge of being a bungler and ineffective would not stick.

The next verse tells us that Paul appealed to his boldness. He said: You are calling me a coward are you? You think I ran because I am afraid. Why do you think I came to you in the first place? I've been scourged, whipped to within an inch of my life in Philippi. I've been put in the stocks. I've been thrown out of town. Everything they could do to me has been done to me and yet I was courageous enough to come into your town and start preaching straightaway. That is courage, not cowardice. How many of us would be in church next Sunday if we were thrown in the stocks and whipped and put in prison because we had attended an act of worship? It would show real courage and boldness if you came back the next Sunday.

In the next verse, Paul appeals to his guilelessness. He appeals to the utter simplicity of his life. He said: We didn't come as crooks. We didn't come with deceitful or dirty motives; we came in utter simplicity. You cannot say otherwise. We came with one motive, and one only. As God has entrusted us with the gospel, so we speak. We came to share with you what he had given us.

Somebody said that being a preacher is one beggar telling another beggar where to find bread. That is the only motive that would stand up in God's sight for preaching. So Paul appeals to his guilelessness and godliness. "God has tested us, God has approved us; God has tried us and if we are acceptable to God to pass the gospel on, then you should be quiet. But God has entrusted us with this message, and he wouldn't have done that unless he had approved us."

He appeals to his gentleness. They had been saying he was a harsh man, a hard man, a tough man. He says, "You know that underneath I was like a nurse with children." That is a very gentle figure. I don't suppose it's the ordinary conception of Paul, but it is the true one – that Paul was a nurse. You see how he cared for babies; you see how he fed them with milk, you see how he cared for them, you see how he saw it through. He was not just interested in counting heads, he was not interested in being the kind of evangelist who got a response and moved on to the next place the next day. He was the kind of evangelist who brought babies into the world and looked after them as gently as a nurse caring for children.

He appealed to his holiness. In v. 10: "You are witnesses and God also, how holy and righteous and blameless was our behaviour to you believers." He appeals to his busyness in v. 9: "You remember night and day we laboured with our hands." In those days in Greece it was thought that if you worked with your hands you were very much lower in the social scale than somebody who worked with their heads. Alas, it is still true that people think that silly way.

If you think like that, let me remind you that for eighteen years Jesus worked with his hands and gave dignity to manual labour. Paul said: You know how night and day, far from coming to get your collections, far from coming to exploit you, we worked night and day, we were not lazy bones. We worked night and day to support ourselves, so that you could never charge us for trying to come to get money from you. And he did support himself. I guess Paul had a pretty tough time sewing those goats' hair tents; it is a tough job, hard on the fingers. If he had not been doing it for a bit, it would be harder still. But every Jewish father in those days used to teach his son some job with his hands, even if he was going to be a scholar, and I think that is not a bad scheme. I knew of one professor of Old Testament theology who did an hour's manual labour every day. He had

33

hands like hams and he did it on the same basis as this verse. Paul tells them that they cannot make that one stick. What else? He could not be accused of compromise, lowering the standard, because he said, "We didn't come to you with words of flattery."

I think one of the most profound insights in Bunyan's *The Pilgrim's Progress* is that the devil keeps appearing to Pilgrim in a different guise, so that Pilgrim never recognises him. The most subtle thing of all is when the devil appears to Pilgrim as the flatterer. Flattery is one of the devil's favourite weapons. A story is told of the preacher who came out of the pulpit and someone said, "That was a magnificent sermon," and he replied, "Yes, the devil told me so just as I left the pulpit." Paul says, "We didn't come to flatter you."

I tell you, as a preacher, it's the easiest thing in the world for a preacher simply to flatter people and simply to tell them how good they are, and he will get a ready audience. Paul did not come to butter people up and to tell them what good people they were, he came to tell them they were sinners, and to walk worthy of the calling of God's kingdom and his glory.

So Paul answers charge after charge, and they could not stick one of them on to him. Whether you preach to a thousand or to one person over the garden fence, you will have to be ready to answer such charges. For they will be made; the devil will not leave you alone. The devil hates the message and therefore, if he cannot twist the message, he will attack the messenger.

A third method of attack is mentioned here: attacking those who receive the message. If there is one thing the devil can do if the preacher is preaching the gospel, it is to stop the people thinking about what is being said, and concentrate their minds on who is saying it. And roast preacher for Sunday lunch is the devil's own design. So you go home and say, "What did you think of him?" The devil rubs his hands and says, "Great, I've got them thinking about the messenger instead of the message." So Paul takes these charges against himself, defends himself, then quietly turns the picture right around and his teaching means this: We thank God that when we came and spoke to you, you did not treat the sermons as human opinion. You did not go home and chew them over as if it was merely a discussion of one man's views; you received our word as it really was, the Word of God. You welcomed warmly the word of God and it began to work in your heart.

The devil would love you to go away and discuss your church or its pastor. But if you go away and receive the Word and let it work in your heart, you have defeated the enemy at the third level.

So these are the three steps: the devil will pervert the message that is being preached, slander the one who preaches it, or keep the attention of those who hear it on the man instead of the message. But, praise God, when the Word is received it begins to work. It is dynamic; something will happen. If the seed of God's Word is in the soil of your heart, and you do not let the devil pluck it out or choke it with weeds, you will find that your life will change. I guarantee you that, because the power is not in the preacher, it is in what he is preaching.

Some years ago, foundations for a new office block were being dug in London, and a Roman temple was unearthed which had been dedicated to the god of the sun, Mithras, the "birthday" of which was on 25th December. The Romans noticed that the sun was getting strong again at that time of year, and that is how Christmas Day came to be on December 25th – because the people of England worshipped the sun god on that day, as did the people of Europe. The Christians said: if you are going to worship the birthday of your god on that day, we are going to celebrate the birthday of ours on the same day. That is how Christmas began. The interesting thing is this: on the altar of that temple in Roman times two thousand years ago, they found the remains of an offering, a harvest festival. There were some grains of wheat on the altar. Dry and dusty, they had been in there for centuries. Somebody took those grains of wheat and put them in some damp soil to see what would happen – and they grew. Little dry grains of wheat after two thousand years of doing nothing, they grew. While I am preaching, I know one of the glorious things that is happening is that I am planting little seeds in your heart. Nothing may happen for years, but it will grow; it has got life in it.

A man lay dying from wounds during the Second World War. A friend leaned beside him and said, "Is there anything I can do for you?"

He said, "No, I'm dying."

"Is there anyone I can send a message to for you?"

"Yes, you can send a message to this man and this address and tell him, 'In my last minutes, what you taught me as a child is helping me to die'" – words to that effect. This man and this address was the address of his old Sunday school teacher. When the message got back to that teacher, he said, "God forgive me, I gave up Sunday school teaching some years ago because I thought I was getting nowhere; I thought it was no use."

As a preacher I am thrilled every Sunday I plant a seed of God's word in hearts. It may lie there dormant for a long time, but one day.... There is life in that seed. The devil does not want that seed to get into your heart. He would much rather you went away and discussed us.

So Paul says, "I thank God you received my word warmly," and it began to work in new believers. It grew up, it germinated. It began to produce fruit and it became life. It was the Word that was life – never believe it was the preacher. It was the message that did it. It always will be.

Now Paul says something pretty rough about his own fellow countrymen and I want to draw one or two lessons from this. The first lesson is this: you can make quite sure that you are receiving the Word of God for the right motive if you suffer for it. If you just receive the gospel because it is going to help you and do you good, you can never be sure that the motive for it was not just selfish. But if you receive the gospel and you pay for it straightaway, and you suffer for it straightaway, you know that *you believed it because it was true*, not because it was nice and not because it was helpful. That is the basic reason for believing that Jesus died for your sins and rose again – not because that helps you. It will but that is not the main reason. If something is true, you are prepared to suffer for it. And if your troubles are greater after you become a Christian than they were before, that proves that you believed it because it was true.

I preach the gospel of our Lord Jesus, not primarily because I believe it is helpful to us, nor because I believe it is nice to hear, nor even because I believe it is comforting, though it is all those things. I preach the gospel because I believe it to be true and I welcome it as the truth and that is why I could not deny it. If one lost everything one cherished, one could not deny the truth of the gospel. If you lost home and family, health and possessions, and lost everything, you would still have to say it is true. Paul says, "I thank God that you received it as the Word of God. You saw it was true, you had to believe it, and as soon as you did you suffered for it, and you were persecuted."

One of the tragedies of Christian suffering is that often it comes from the least likely source, from those who claim to be nearest to God. That is why the greatest enemy to Christianity in England is religion. One day I preached in a London church at one of those annual, official occasions.

The unreality of it was almost unbearable and I cringed. It was an odd occasion but it was an opportunity to preach the Word, and I went because I believe if a door opens, then let us go through and preach the gospel. I knew that those who had organised the service, though they would claim to be Christians, and they doffed their hats to God when that was right and proper, were just not liking the gospel. I could sense it. The atmosphere went cooler and cooler, and the total silence about the sermon afterwards from the organizers could be felt. The incredible thing is that two adults spoke warmly and realistically about what had been said. One was a Jew and one was a humanist; neither of them was a professed Christian believer and my heart was warm to them. It was real – and often it is those who should be nearest to God who sometimes prove to be your greatest enemies.

That is what happened when Jesus came to the chosen people of God who had been prepared for fifteen hundred years for this moment. He came to the people who claimed to be the religious leaders of the world, and what did they do? They killed him. Why? Because he tried to get them nearer to God and he spoke the Word of God. Some young people know what I am talking about. They go home to their parents, and those parents had them christened and took them to church and sent them to Sunday school. You would have thought they would be thrilled to hear the news when their children said, "I've been converted! I'm a Christian!" Too often the response is: you've got religious-mania like the rest of them. Such young people are then surprised and hurt. "They had me done as a child, aren't they thrilled that now it's fulfilled? Aren't they over the moon that I've come to Christ?" The tragedy is that churchianity is the biggest enemy of Christianity. Is that not true? It is those who claim to be near to God but refuse to be brought nearer who become the greatest enemies of the gospel.

Jesus came to bring people to God, to bring Israel to God, and they killed him. It was not just one stray offence; it was a fixed attitude. They had killed the prophets all the way up to him. They attacked every man of God who had come to them with a message from God. This was all of a piece with their attitude. "It has gone on," Paul says, "ever since they turned us out of their country," and they did. If you had been a Christian in Jerusalem in the early years of the Christian church, you would have had to leave Jerusalem, to run for your life and take your kids with you. Paul says, "They're even jealous because I am giving what they claim to have to Gentiles."

After the Yom Kippur War, the chief Rabbi of Israel called on the Jews to repent of their exclusiveness. What he meant was this – something that Jesus said to the Jews: "You will neither enter into the kingdom yourselves, nor will you let others come in." The tragedy of it is that if we refuse a deeper experience of the Lord, we are jealous of others getting it. That is the tragedy of the Jewish race and it is also the tragedy of other people today.

May I speak very frankly? I may have been a Christian for many years. I may have been a faithful church member. I may have served the Lord faithfully, and then some young person seems to come into a blessing that I have never had; I am jealous. It is tragic when the devil gets hold of you like this. Because I refuse to go further in the Spirit, I do not want others to because it shows me up. And I close my heart, and I do not receive God's further word.

Paul was saying that was what happened to the Jews, and it was they who opposed what God was doing – it was the chosen people of God who opposed it, the very people who should have been nearer to him who were keeping others away. It was the very people who were prepared for him, who would not have him. It was the very people who should

39

have been telling you about Jesus who were angry with me for sharing the gospel with you. It is a sad situation. But Paul has switched the whole picture and he is saying: "Don't go home thinking about the messenger, go home asking, 'Am I refusing the message?' Because if I am, I will become antagonistic to those who accept it."

Whenever God says something new through a messenger, we can either receive it and grow and let it produce fruit, or we can refuse it, in which case we will find ourselves resentful that others received it and are going past us in the race that we're called to run. So Paul is defending the message, defending the messenger, and defending those who listen to the message. The devil is foiled at all three points, and the Word of God has free sway, and the Word of God speaks and is planted in good soil, and the church grows in faith, and hope and love develop, and the devil gnashes his teeth – but the church grows. Said Jesus to Peter, "I will build my church, and the gates of hades can't stop it," and that is precisely what is happening now.

Let us take three solemn warnings from this passage. One: never twist the message of the gospel; just give it as it is. There is only one gospel, don't let the devil spoil it. You cannot improve on it, just pass it on. What Samuel Chadwick said about the Bible can be said about the gospel also. He said, "I never defend the Bible. For the Bible is like a lion in a cage. All I do is open the door and let it out." Don't defend the gospel, just open the door; let it out. People may say, "It's a foolish story," people may say, "It's a silly story," people may say, "You can't expect me to believe that." Don't argue, just let it out; let them face the lion. Let the message get through; let the power of the gospel be seen.

Warning number two: even Christians can fall into this; don't let the devil make you one of the slanderers of his messengers. It is his own device to get you thinking about the preacher instead of what was said. Warning number three: don't resist. If God says something new to you in any service, calls you to some new step to take, to some new venture of fellowship, say: "I'm going further and you're coming with me." Go with him, receive the message, let it go into your heart. Because the tragedy is that if you don't, you will very soon be an enemy of those who do, and you will fight them.

So let us take these warnings to heart and let the Word of God dwell richly in our hearts by faith.

3

Read 1 Thessalonians 2:17–3:13

PRESENT RELATIONS

1. Frustration (2:17–3:5)
   a. Not coming – Satan preventing
   b. Not hearing – Timothy despatched

2. Satisfaction (3:6–13)
   a. Hearing – Timothy returning
   b. Coming and God allowing

I do not know if you realise what a wonderful thing it was when Paul wrote to the Thessalonians, maybe the very first part of the New Testament to be written. Paul thought he was just writing a letter, but that little thing suddenly became so important. The personal letter became part of God's Word. You have no idea just how much God can use a little thing. Thank God that Paul wrote the letter. I am so glad that most of the New Testament is in the form of epistles because letters are so personal. Humanly speaking, most of the New Testament was almost written accidentally or incidentally – just letters dashed off in a moment to meet a need, and in these letters there shines through the affection and relationships that are formed in Jesus Christ which come to mean so much to us.

Do you realise that twelve months earlier Paul did not know a single person at Thessalonica? Now he is writing to them and saying: away from you I feel bereaved. It is a demonstration of how deep relationships are given to us in Jesus Christ – new brothers and sisters, a new family to which we belong. So real are these new relationships that I think most Christians would agree that within a very short time of knowing Christ you feel closer to your fellow believers than to your own unconverted relatives. In this passage I read the deep affection and love, the heartthrob of Paul, shine through.

Was Paul an evangelist, a missionary, a pastor, a teacher, an elder, or what? I have come to the conclusion he was the whole lot rolled into one. We can all learn from him a very great deal about relationships with those we are seeking to help. Here is a spiritual father writing to his children. I am so encouraged that Paul is honest enough to say that sometimes he was in the depths of depression and anxiety about the work of God, and at other times he was on the top of a mountain, so bubbly with joy he had just to put it down on paper.

You know, we sometimes get the idea that the ideal Christian life is one that just stays beautifully even, with no ups and downs. I do not find much of that in the New Testament – not even in the life of Jesus. There are times when Jesus wept and times when he exulted in spirit and said, "I thank you Father that you're revealing things to babes and sucklings that are hidden from the wise." So there are depths of anxiety in the Christian life and service, and there are heights of joy. We are going to see what causes this kind of emotional up and down, how it is put right and how we can cope with it.

First of all, let us highlight the desire Paul expresses in 2:17–20. Remember that he had to leave Thessalonica in a hurry, under cover of darkness. What would you feel if next Sunday you heard that your church leader had done a midnight flit on Tuesday? All sorts of rumours would go around. People would say, "There's something he's running away from." Paul had to do just that. The civic situation was so tense that it was decided by the leaders of that little church that they had better get Paul out of there quietly and quickly. So, under cover of darkness, some of the brethren sent him off to Berea and the next Sunday when they came together to worship, their leader had gone. Some people probably said, "Well, he's a 'fly by night' and he doesn't really think much about us." But Paul is letting them know: "Listen, I want to tell you that even though I left you in body, my heart stayed with you. My heart has never left you." When you have come into a spiritual family, and have brothers and sisters in Christ, wherever your body goes, your heart stays.

Paul's heart stayed there – he was not a man who was only interested in what happened while he was there and lost interest as soon as he had gone. He longed to see them and he wanted to be with them. You notice he says, "Even though my heart stayed with you I wanted my body to join my heart. I wanted to see your face." There is a very real sense in which because we are in the flesh, in the body, even if our heart may be with people that is not enough. It is not satisfying – our bodies must be where our hearts are. We long to be with people physically. So Paul was saying that was how he really felt about them. Here is a man who really has a deep love for people.

But he says that he could not get back because Satan stopped him coming. I would love to be able to ask Paul a few questions – for a quarter of an hour or more! The tragedy is that when I finally get to him I won't have any more questions. I would like to ask, for example, "How did Satan stop you getting back to them?" It doesn't say. An even deeper question I would like to ask him would be: "Look Paul, there were times in your life when you were stopped going places and then you said it was the Holy Spirit who stopped you. Now you are saying Satan stopped you. How do you know when it is which?" Paul seemed to be so sure that he could say, "The Holy Spirit forbade me to go to Bithynia, he hindered me from going into Asia." But now he says that Satan hindered him from going to Thessalonica. How did he know? Because sometimes I am stopped doing something and I do not know whether it is the Lord, or the devil, or who. I would love to put Paul in the hot seat and say, "How do you know?" The one thing we can be certain of is this: he was quite sure when it was Satan stopping him. He was absolutely sure when it was the old devil putting a blockage. Literally he says, "Satan put a roadblock in my path and I couldn't get through to you."

Shall I tell you why Satan does this? I don't know how he was doing it, and I don't know how Paul knew he was doing it, but I do know why he did it. If Satan can keep Christians apart, he will. If Satan can keep teacher and pupil apart, he will. If Satan can keep someone who can meet the spiritual needs of a group of Christians away from them he will, and he will do anything at all. So I do not know if Satan was causing Paul sickness or whether Satan was causing people to oppose his passage through the frontier, from one section of Greece to another but I know why – to separate Christians from one another when they could have been building each other up.

Paul has a double desire. He says: "I want to be present with you on earth and I want to be proud of you in heaven." There is one reunion of Christians that Satan will never be able to stop. He may stop me meeting a Christian on earth but he cannot stop me meeting him in heaven. The reunion to which Paul now looks forward! He is saying: even if Satan keeps me away from you for the rest of my life, I will meet you there, and he cannot interfere with that.

I remember saying to our pastor friend who lived in a Communist country, "I do hope that you'll be able to come and visit Guildford." He replied, "They've taken away my passport and they won't reconsider it for another three years." I said to him, "Well, will you come then in three years' time to Guildford? We'd love to have you there." He just said with a smile, "I might be in heaven before then, and they don't need to give me a visa to get there." The man was free – he was looking forward to the one meeting of Christians that Satan can do nothing about. He may stop us being present with each other on earth, but he cannot stop us meeting the Lord in the air when Jesus Christ comes back.

Paul not only wants to be present with his people on earth, he wants to be proud of them on that day. Paul bursts out: you are our hope, our joy, our glory, our crown. The word he uses for "crown" we would call a gold medal. It is the laurel wreath used for the races in those days. To Jesus he would say those people were his crown or crowning achievement. When you face Jesus, what will be your crown? What will

47

be your glory?

I tell you, there are many things that people are putting their hopes in now which, when they meet Jesus, will not be their hope. There are many things that people glory in now, which you will not glory in on that day. You may have passed all your exams, you may have built up a big business, you may have got the house just how you want it. They will not be your glory in that day. In that day your glory will be the number of people you have brought nearer to Christ – it is as simple as that. They are your hope of being proud in that day. They will be your joy on that day; they will be your glory. There is a legitimate pride. How bursting you will feel with the right kind of pride if you can face Jesus in that day and say, "You see these people? I helped to bring them to you, Lord."

Paul uses a very interesting word for the coming of our Lord Jesus. It is the first time the word is ever used, as far as we know, of that coming. It is a Greek word that means a royal visit. When we stand before the Lord, our hope in glory will be those we have led nearer to Christ. That is Paul's heart, ambition, desire. The apostle wants to be present with Christians on earth and to be proud of them in heaven. If you have that same desire then you will understand the rest of the letter.

3:1-5 Secondly we look at vv.1–5. There is Paul's anxiety, that got him so depressed he said he got to the point where he could bear it no longer. What anxiety could get Paul as low as that? He was really down. He had moved on from Thessalonica to Berea, going further south. Now he was in Athens, that pagan place.

It makes you think of the pessimistic, intellectual areas that you get in great universities, where at first you feel in a sense embarrassed to be coming with the simple gospel of Jesus Christ into that place. How alone you feel! How am

I going to tackle these great brains? How am I going to get into this world? Paul felt like that at Athens.

He had with him an interesting companion, a rather timid, shy young man with delicate health – just the opposite of Paul temperamentally, physically and every way. Paul and Timothy were most unusual companions, yet between them was a deep bond. They relied heavily on each other. The Lord means us not to try it alone but to have someone we can rely on. Paul and Timothy came to Athens, and in the face of all this intellectualism, antagonism and paganism, they clung to each other for support. But Paul had a greater anxiety than how to meet the needs of Athens. His anxiety was about what was happening at Thessalonica: I know they are going through it – how are they standing up to it?

They say no news is good news, but I do not think that is true. I think that even the worst news is better than no news. I have found that with patients. Doctors will tell you that to tell a patient nothing is worse than telling them the worst. They can cope with bad news, but no news is horrible. There is the strain of silence.

Paul had to bear this. Here is an evangelist who is not just interested in how many people start the Christian life, but how they stand, what they are doing twelve months later, and how they are coping with opposition and persecution.

So Paul said he was prepared to remain all alone and send Timothy to find out. He could bear it no longer and had to find out what was happening. The two things he was worried about were these: first that they would be discouraged by distress. He had warned them. Thank God for honest preachers and evangelists who say, "You come to Christ and you will suffer. Come to Christ and your troubles will begin. You come to Christ and you're in for a very tough time." Paul says, "In Thessalonica, I told you, again and again, that through much tribulation you will enter the kingdom, it will be big trouble. I warned you that this was coming." It is one thing to know that in your head, but another thing to have it happen to you.

I warn you, though in a lesser degree in this Christianised land, that still for every Christian life is going to be a battle until they cross to the other side. It is tough to be a Christian in this world, because it is not a Christian world and you don't belong to it. It belongs to Satan, the prince of this world, the god of this world. It really belongs to God ultimately, but Satan has got hold of it. So for the Christian it is going to be tough. Paul said it repeatedly and they had heard it. But now he knew it was happening.

I have talked to many new Christians and discovered that the honeymoon lasts on average two to three months, during a kind of ride on a cloud – and you think you are in for a comfortable ride to glory. Then, between the end of the second and the beginning of the fourth month, you just go "bang". I don't know if you remember when that happened to you. I don't know if you remember your first really tough time. Perhaps the opposition came from the most unexpected quarter. And it is tough to be a Christian.

Paul is also worried that not only will human opposition come, and human problems of relationships, but behind all that there is someone who can exploit that situation to the full. The apostle is afraid that they are also being tempted by the tempter. After all, Satan has prevented Paul going again and again. The trouble is that when there is opposition and the going gets tough, Satan whispers horrible things in your ear. He says, "It's not worth it." He says, "You didn't think it was going to be as bad as this, did you? Well of course it is your own silly fault, you started being a Christian." He whispers away to you. The tempter tempts and he can exploit that kind of situation. Paul was a very good evangelist so he had to find out. He was not content to leave them.

3:6-9

Now, thirdly, his delight: vv. 6–9. There is nothing more encouraging and thrilling to a Christian worker than to know that someone he has started off is still going. What a joy to know it lasts, they have stood firm even though they have had it tough. The tempter has not got hold of them. God has got hold of them even more firmly because it has been tough. I would just ask you a simple question. Think of the person who was most instrumental in leading you to the Lord. Would your present spiritual state be a source of joy and delight to them? Have you ever thought that way? Have you ever thought of writing and telling them how you are getting on?

The only time that the word "gospel" is used for anything other than the good news about Jesus Christ is in this passage. Paul says: Timothy came back with a gospel for me, a good news for me. The great news was that your faith and your love were as strong as ever, and that you missed me as much as I did you, and you want to see me as much as I want to see you. Paul says, "We now live. You have put new life into us to know that you are going on, to know that you are standing firm." This really does put new life into people.

If we who are Christian workers are not careful, we hear most about those who do not go on. We hear about the problems, the backsliders, those who are getting into difficulties. Sometimes we have had a week of it, hearing of those who have got into problems, those who are backsliding and those who are getting into difficulties. There are few things that lower the morale of Christian workers as quickly. But when you hear of someone who has gone on, who is standing, and who has developed in faith and love, it puts new life into you. You feel, "Right, let's go out for another, let's go after someone else." It is all worthwhile – to know that your children stand firm in the faith; it strengthens you for living.

The faithfulness of Paul's converts was a matter of life and death to Paul. He says, "I was dying in spirit because I heard nothing of you. Now we live, if you stand fast in the Lord. It's life to us to know this." Then he bursts out into thanksgiving, giving glory where glory is due. He can hardly find the words for the Lord and he pours out thanksgiving and says, "Lord, thank you, thank you, thank you." This letter must have been written as soon as Timothy got back because it is bursting. If you read it in a modern translation you will get the emotions of it even more. After months of anxiety – it is alright, they are going on, they are as strong as ever. So his delight at it, his joy, is very obvious.

A very practical outworking of this might be that you get in touch with the person who led you to the Lord and tell them, "I'm going on, I'm going on." You might put new life into them and help them to go on themselves.

The next thing to mention is Paul's dissatisfaction. You would have thought with all that good news he had that, having been so thrilled he might have said: "Great, I can cross them off my prayer list. Great, I can stop thinking about them. I can get on with Athens now, and Corinth, and all the rest—that is marvellous; I leave them to it, they are going on well." Not so—Paul was a man who was never content with less than the best; never content until people had all that God had for them.

So this great news Timothy had brought made Paul pray for two things. He prayed even more that he might come to them and that he might be able to make up what was lacking in their faith: I want even more for you than you've got if you're going on well – that is a strange reaction. He is not satisfied with the good news, he still wants more!

First he prayed that he might be able to see them. That prayer was answered five years later. Are you prepared to pray for a thing for five years? He had to pray for five years until the power of God broke down Satan's obstacles, and he got through to Thessalonica. So Paul met them again on earth. His other prayer was an intriguing one. The word he uses for making up what is lacking is a word that a fisherman uses for mending a gash or tear in a net. I want to make a horrible pun now, which I think you may remember: there are two sorts of Christians and the difference between them is one letter. They are both holy, and one is spelled h-o-l-e-y and the other is spelled h-o-l-y. Paul wants to fill the holes in their faith and to be complete in faith, to have everything that God has for them.

There are still gaps in their experience. We shall find out about some of them and they are surprising gaps, things we would not have thought would need to be said in a Christian fellowship. Paul wants Christians to be unblamable in holiness, to close the gaps, mend the nets, repair what is lacking in the believers' faith until they are complete people. The English word "holy" comes from an old Anglo-Saxon word *halig*, which means "whole, complete so there's nothing lacking – everything's there."

Some people like to dismantle watches and such like and maybe lose parts. God wants to make *us* work properly and so he wants to get every part in, he wants to get the Christian complete, he wants a holy man or woman who is increasing in love and abounding in love. Two words which Paul uses mean "increasing within us" and "overflowing out of us". A holy person is someone who is so increased that he or she overflows. It is a positive picture of holiness, not negative. It is of someone who is increasing in these things and overflowing in these things, so Paul prays for that. Once again he gets back to the main subject of the two letters to the Thessalonians: the royal visit of Jesus. He wants people to be unblamable in holiness at the coming of our Lord Jesus.

Let us tie those two ends together. Paul was teaching that

there are two things a Christian needs if they are going to welcome our Lord's coming. One is that they come with hope in others whom they have brought to Christ. The second is that they come with holiness in themselves. When the Lord comes back and says, "What have you done on earth?" If you are able to point to other people as your hope you can say, "Lord, I helped to bring these to yourself; these are my crown, these are my reward; these are my joy. And if you are a net without a single hole, a whole Christian, unblamable in holiness, then believe me, Jesus will look at your face and say with a smile, "Well done good and faithful servant. Enter into the joy of your Lord."

Do you want to be ready for the Lord's coming? Doesn't it put it in a different perspective? Doesn't it make you look at all the things you do in a different light? Doesn't it make you alter your scale of values? These are the two things you will need to face him properly – other people brought to him and yourself fit to meet him. Let me add one word for those who are not Christians: until you know and love the Lord Jesus Christ you won't even meet him at his coming. One day you will meet him as judge, but you won't meet him with joy.

4

Read 1 Thessalonians 4:1–12

A. IN MARRIAGE – INCORRUPTIBLE (1–8)
1. Not passionate lust
2. But pure love

B. IN CHURCH – INCLUSIVE (9–10)
1. Local (Thessalonica)
2. Regional (Macedonia)

C. IN SOCIETY – INOFFENSIVE (11–12)
1. Demure – live quietly
2. Discreet – mind own business
3. Diligent – work with hands

When the compass was invented, mariners thought their problems of navigation were over, and now there was a fixed point to which ships could refer. Then they discovered that the magnetic North Pole was not in the same place as the true North Pole and began to have to make adjustments. Later it was discovered that the magnetic North Pole is moving all the time and has wandered over the Arctic Circle, and that what is north now magnetically, will not be north in ten or twenty years. Furthermore, when the first iron ships were built, the compasses in those ships went haywire and pointed in all directions, having to be shielded and protected against the iron of the vessel. But once a compass is protected, and checked, and tested, and constantly re-tested it is a fine aid to navigation to keep a ship on course.

Built into every man, woman, and child there is a compass that we call the conscience. Everyone has some sense of right and wrong, some things they say are right and some they say are wrong. But our conscience is an inaccurate guide to the course that we need to steer through life. It can be affected by many different factors, like a compass in an iron ship. Our conscience can be influenced by our own desires, our own intuitions, our own impulses and our own affections.

We also know that our consciences can be conditioned by what is happening around us, and that if we tie our conscience to the society in which we live, we will steer a very erratic course. The conscience, like a compass, needs to be protected, tested, checked and constantly reset if we are going to steer a straight course through life. Most of us have a conscience that is too largely conditioned by the way we were brought up, and the things we feel guilty about are those our parents taught us to feel guilty about. Therefore, there is the need constantly to find "true north". It may be summed up in a sentence: if your conscience is aligned to Christ and to him alone, you will steer a true course. If your own flesh interferes with it, you will go all over the place. If the desires and ambitions of society around you influence that compass, you will steer all over the place. But once you have got in line with the teaching, example and mind and Spirit of Christ, and constantly check your compass accordingly, you will steer straight, live straight and steer the right course through life. That is why it is vital to check your conscience constantly, to bring it in line with what the Lord says is the course.

It is not just enough to win people to Christ and baptise them. Jesus knew it would not be enough. Even after you have become a baptised Christian, your conscience is still not reliable enough as a guide to all your decisions and conduct. That is why Jesus said, "Go into all the world and make disciples. Baptise them in the name of the Father, the Son, and the Holy Spirit." That is not the end of your job – in fact, it is just the beginning. Then: "... teach them to observe all that I have commanded you." Constantly line them up with God's will. Constantly tell them what is the straight course. I thank God for those evangelists who know that they must not only be evangelists, they must be catechists. They must not only bring people to Christ, they must then begin the slow and sometimes long task of getting those compasses right – teaching, teaching, teaching. This is important even after you have progressed a considerable way in the Christian life.

We have seen that Paul, writing to the Thessalonians, is writing to a successful church. He is writing to a church which is full of faith, hope and love. He is writing to a church that has a reputation that has spread far and wide, a church where people are turning from their idols and turning to the living God and waiting for Jesus to come from heaven. He is writing to a church that we would say does not need anything, a church of which we might say: "That church is alright, we can move on and start another."

Not so Paul, writing to this successful, growing church in which people are being converted and standing firm, in which there is a lot of love of the brethren, a church which is sending the gospel out and evangelising the surrounding district, and Paul says, "I want to come back to you to mend the holes" [the literal word], "to supply what is lacking." The apostle wants to come and teach them the way, to come and check their compass – to come and deal with some very practical things concerned with their course in life. For this is the will of God: your sanctification.

Many people come to me and say, "I'm trying to find the will of God for my life." Perhaps it sounds facetious but I am tempted to reply, "Well, you should have no difficulty in doing that." You don't need to look any further than this verse in 1 Thessalonians 4 to find the will of God for your life: "This is the will of God, your sanctification." Until you have found that part of the will of God there is no point in asking for any more. In other words, God is far more interested in my character than in my career.

The tragedy is that when people say, "I'm trying to find the will of God for my life," they are thinking of career – where they should be and what they should be doing. God is far more interested in *how* you are doing it. He is interested not so much in what you achieve as in what you become. "This is the will of God, your sanctification" is a truth that applies to every Christian, be they old or young, men or women, clever or not so clever, rich or poor – for every Christian the will of God for your life is your sanctification. The word means, quite simply, the process of becoming whole or holy, so that the gaps are closed, the loose ends are tied together – so that you are complete in Christ.

This is our subject now: holiness. I wonder what that word conveys to you. It is a musty word that unfortunately speaks to some people of a very private and personal thing that is best pursued by oneself, preferably shut into some cell of a monastery or a convent where you can get that halo polished. That is the kind of impression I get from this word "holiness". Nothing could be further from the truth. We shall find that holiness is a very practical thing, concerned with how you get on in your home, your church, your community and where you work.

We will discover that you can never be holy by yourself (that is a discovery worth making) and that holiness is primarily concerned with relationships. There are three areas of relationship that we are going to deal with here: (i) the relationships between men and women, (ii) between Christian and Christian, and (iii) between a Christian and his neighbour in the community. Holiness, if it is to be anything, has to be worked out right there in your marriage, your church and the community. So we are going to look at these very practical relationships.

This is the will of God, even your sanctification. That means that if I live for selfishness then I am against the will of God and I am constantly going to be running into trouble. But if my ambition is to be sanctified, I am with God and he is with me and I have got heaven itself on my side. If you choose an unholy life then, frankly, you are on your own. The devil might help you a bit, but as far as God is concerned you are on your own.

This word will cut deep, for it is the Word of God and it is sharper than any two-edged sword. In all three areas Paul is saying to the Thessalonians: you have brought too much of your pre-Christian life into your Christian life; you are still living partially in the world that you left behind, that you buried when you were baptised. You may be full of faith, you may be full of hope, you may have abounding love but you have still got some other things that you should not have, that you should have left behind long ago. It may seem strange to you when I mention them that these things should need to be mentioned in a church, but if you know society today, and if you know the church today, and if you know yourself today, you know that the Word of God is still very necessary.

So let us look at the first one: the relationship between men and women. Has it ever struck you as strange that half the people on earth are male and half are female? It would do if you had come from another world where that did not apply. It is part of God's created order that we are men and women and that all of us are sexual beings. He made us so, and we cannot deny that, and it is the source of some of our greatest agonies and some of our highest ecstasies. It is one of the great driving forces in our life, and most people, if they are honest, would say they have difficulty in handling it. Paul is going to deal very practically with what happens when it is uncontrolled by God's Holy Spirit.

The best way to introduce this, and the most practical, is to tell you what was happening in the world in Paul's day. It is almost a carbon copy of the situation in which we have been having to live these last few years. Let me begin with Greece. Here is a statement from a Greek philosopher as he said it: "We have prostitutes for pleasure, mistresses for day-to-day needs of the body, and wives to beget our children." There was no surprise at his statement, which was simply an observation of life. As long as a man supported his wife and kids, society was not the slightest bit worried about how many affairs he had. The result was, of course, that marriage was regarded in a very low way by the Greeks. When you study Greek mythology you find that they were guilty of making God in their own image, and the gods did exactly the same. They came to earth and philandered.

Now the Roman attitude was just about the same. In 520 years of the Republic of Rome there was not one single divorce, but when the empire began then that picture changed. By the time Paul got to Thessalonica you changed your partners at any whim. If you found somebody else more attractive, you said goodbye to your wife and you picked up the new one. In fact, one Roman said, "We marry in order to divorce and we divorce in order to marry." I think it is Juvenal who mentions one woman who boasted of having got through eight husbands in five years – and it is almost like reading the latest column in a tabloid newspaper.

What about the Jews? Were they any better? We find that one of the biggest problems in our Lord's own day was this matter of changing partners. The strict rabbi says, "You must not divorce your wife except for adultery", but for every strict rabbi there were half a dozen lax rabbis who said, "If your wife burns your breakfast, if she has a loud enough voice for the neighbours to hear her, you can divorce her." I am telling you the literal truth, which is why when they came to Jesus with questions they asked him about this very thing. Now lying behind this situation is a very important question, and you will realise that this is the situation that is coming rapidly here. The question behind the whole situation is this: is love something that controls me, or is it something that I control? Many of the songs we hear on radio and television are saying that love is something you cannot control – it happens to you and it is something you fall into and out of, not something you build up. And if you fall out of it you cannot help that any more than falling into it. Therefore, when you fall out of it that is the end of the relationship and there is no point in hanging on to it. This is the question that Paul is raising. He is saying: are your desires for the opposite sex under control or in control? Which is it to be?

He makes it quite clear that into that ancient world came a totally new viewpoint on love, something so different that one historian has said that the early Christians were like a cluster of snowdrops growing on a foul rubbish heap. The new viewpoint they brought in was this: that love is to be under our control, not over it, and that there is a new view of marriage coming in. It is not that you have fallen in love and cannot help it, and that you will marry this person – you will just agree to live together and then if you fall out of love you separate. It is not that. The new viewpoint that came in was this: let each man hold his wife to himself, be loyal to her, and put loyalty into the attraction he has felt and turn it into a different kind of love.

Paul is saying that uncontrolled desires, subject to no restraints and controlling us, is simply lust, whether it is inside or outside marriage. Both are wrong in Paul's sight according to this chapter. If marriage is no more than legalised lust, it will break down. Paul is saying that sooner or later it will break down and you will sin against your partner. You will find another wife who is more attractive than your own and you will go after her and you will sin against her husband. Or if you give way to uncontrolled desire for a girl who is not married, you still defraud your brother – defrauding him because you are robbing her future husband of what he might have had. This then is the new standard that came into the world in Christ's earthly ministry.

In other words, there is no room whatever in Christian standards for affairs. That is why the Christian marriage service is so meaningful. When I marry a young couple I do not say, "Do you love each other?" I do not say, "Have you fallen in love?" I do not say, "What are your heart feelings towards each other?" We assume that they have fallen in love. We assume that they are attracted to each other. We assume that they like each other. What we are really asking is: will you add loyalty to your love? Will you be faithful to her as long as you both live? Will you cherish her, will you hold her till death do you part? Are you prepared to have the Christian love for her and hold on? That's a big question to ask.

When they reply to the question, they don't say, "I feel like it," or, "I think I will." They say, "I will." This has cynically been called the longest sentence in the English language. But it is precisely that – a total commitment. That is a new standard that was brought, and so Paul says you cannot be holy as long as love controls you. When you control love, you can. Now one of the serious things he says here is that if a man is guilty of defrauding his brother in this regard, then God is the avenger of that brother. The brother will not need to do anything himself, God will avenge it. That is a terrible sentence: to have God taking revenge on you for what you have done to someone else.

That is the first area of holiness that Paul mentions. Is that not surprising? Did you think that Paul, when he talked about sanctification and holiness, was going to get right up into the clouds of meditation, even prayer? Did you think he was going to go right up into some holy subject when he mentioned it? On the contrary, he has just come right down to earth and talked about the mutual attraction between men and women.

So frightened have people been of this power, so aware have they been of how difficult it is to control, that many have jumped to the opposite extreme and said that the only safe way is celibacy. Paul himself was celibate. He was possibly a widower. The evidence points that way because nobody who trained to be a rabbi remained unmarried. You had to be married even to become a rabbi, and he did. But Paul had a very sound view of marriage. He taught that the answer is not celibacy but marriage of the right kind – not legalised lust but holy matrimony in which you add loyalty to your love, and that is the answer to it, and that is holiness in *holy* matrimony.

Now we move to the second area of which Paul writes. Again it is utterly practical: your relationship within the church to your fellow Christians. A man who thinks he is holy and does not love his fellow Christians is self-deluded. It has rightly been said that there is an ugly kind of "faultlessness" which is always raising its head – a kind of "holiness" which knows nothing of love but consists in spiritual isolation, censoriousness, holding up one's head and shaking off the dust of one's feet against brethren in conceit and condescension, in sanctimonious separateness from the freedom of common life, as though one were too good for the company which God has given you, and that is an abomination in God's sight. Purity without love is not holiness. What is it then? It is Pharisaism. Jesus said that unless your righteousness can exceed that, you won't even see the kingdom of heaven. This is the glorious truth – that holiness is not just a negative. There are certainly negatives in holiness. There are some things that are just out for the Christian and changing your spouse is one of them. But if it is just negatives it is not holiness, it is sanctimoniousness. The will of God for you is not sanctimoniousness, it is sanctification, and sanctification is love—it is positive, it involves affection and warmth.

This is the proof someone is a Christian. The Bible says, "Hereby we know that we have passed from death to life". Why? Because we sing heartily? No. Because we know our Bible back to front? No, it is *because we love the brethren*, and holiness is loving each other. True holiness is to be in a relationship of love with your wife or husband, and with your fellow Christians as one family under God. That is why I mentioned that you can never be holy by yourself. Do you realise that the Bible makes it impossible for a Christian to be holy without other Christians? It is not a thing you can pursue by yourself as a private ambition. It is something you have to pursue in a family circle with your fellow brothers and sisters in Christ. Holiness is cold without this, but with this it becomes a warm and attractive thing.

How far is that love of the brethren to go? The answer is as far as you can reach. The centre of it must be the local church of which you are a member, and that is where you learn to love. The three loves a Christian must have are: loving God with all his heart, his mind, his soul, his strength, loving his neighbour as himself, and loving one another – his fellow Christians. The third I find the more difficult and I guess people find it the more difficult with me, because you cannot choose your family. I have mentioned elsewhere that I was the middle child of three: elder sister, then me, then the younger. What a bad arrangement! I was not the oldest, so I did not have the authority. I was not the youngest, so I was not spoiled. I was just stuck in the middle without any other boys to play football with. So when I got married what happened? We had a girl, then a boy, and then a girl. Now my son felt the way I did. You don't choose your brothers and sisters. You are part of a family, born into it. You choose your wife or husband and then you remain faithful. But you do not choose your children and the children do not choose each other but you learn to love as a family.

Holiness consists in learning to love even that fellow Christian you do not like, until people can look at a church and say, "See how these Christians love one another. Just look at the relationship, look at the affection; look at the warmth." Nothing can damage a church's cause more than members within the church criticising other members within the church. In the world's eyes that finishes a church off. So Paul can say: I know that you love one another, but I want you to do so more and more. The centre of your circle of love for the brethren is the local church.

What is the circumference? There isn't one. It must go

out to your Christian brethren as far as your love can reach. Paul says, "I thank God that you not only love each other in Thessalonica, I have heard that you love every Christian in Macedonia, but I want you to do so more and more. I want your love to go further than that." A Christian's love if it is tied into the local church alone is not holiness. Holiness means I love everybody in this church. Holiness means I love every Christian wherever I meet them, whatever their denominational label. Holiness means I love every Christian in the whole world when I meet them. Jesus is holy and he loves every one of his brethren, and holiness is to be like Jesus.

Now the third area in which we are to be holy is right out there in the world. I want you to realise that if you shut yourself in a monastery or a convent, or shut yourself just in your bedroom, and shut yourself off in a kind of ghetto, if you just go to church, if you don't have any contacts outside Christian circles, if you have no interests that bring you into a relationship with non-Christians, then you cannot be holy. For holiness, as we see now in this third area, is to be right in the world relating to people – alongside them. Holiness is not a call to come out of the world but to go into the world and be different. A call to be separate is not a call to be geographically separate.

Jesus said, "Go into all the world," he never told us to get out of it. On the last night before he died, he said, "Father I sanctify myself," which means: I am going to go through with the cross. I am yours. I am going to line up with your will. To please his Father was Christ's ambition: "I sanctify myself, and Father I want you to sanctify these disciples of mine. I do not pray that you will take them out of the world." So many Christians have made the mistake of thinking that the further they got from the world the holier they were.

I remember someone sitting in a house with plush carpets

up to your knees, you know, that kind of house. Gigantic television set, grand piano. This person told me that they were not worldly – they had never been to a cinema, never been to a theatre. Worldliness does not consist in how many miles you are from sinners, it is being in the world, right in a dirty world and staying clean. That, of course, will require the Holy Spirit – because have you ever noticed that dirt is infectious but cleanliness is not? Dirt passes on from one to another, but cleanliness never does. If you shake hands with a dirty hand, does that make it clean? Never, but Christ wants us right in the world.

Now look at the three things he says now. When you are in the world, whether in factory, shop, office or wherever, when you are right in the world rubbing shoulders with non-Christians, I beg of you, do not envy those who bought a big house in the country and stacked it with cushions and are just living a holy life there. They have shut themselves off, I believe, from being holy. I beg you, don't think that if you can get into a Christian firm where everybody is a Christian, and you have a Christian boss and Christian colleagues, that you are going to find yourself being holy. You will find maybe just the opposite. It is right where you are.

What are the three things you will need to be holy in that world? They are extraordinary. You will need to be quiet, you will need to mind your own business, and you will need to work hard. Now who says the Bible isn't practical? Minding your own business is holiness according to the Bible here. Paul, in a paradoxical statement, writes, "I want you to be restless to be still. Don't get any rest until you are quiet." He is saying: I want you to live quietly.

What does he mean? There are some people who are always drawing attention to themselves; they are always so excitable, or hysterical, silly or exhibitionist – always drawing attention to themselves so that you always know they are there. Paul says holiness consists in being unobtrusive, quiet, calm, getting on with the job, maybe so that you are hardly noticed. I am not sure that he would be sympathetic with going to work in a car covered with stickers and handing out tracts as soon as you get in.

Paul says that we are first to be quiet; live quietly, not noisily, not wanting to make a splash, not wanting to make a show, not wanting to be the life and soul of the party. A holy person lives quietly.

Secondly, a holy person in the world minds his own business. The opposite is to be a busybody, always telling everybody else what to do, interfering in what they are doing. Busybodiness and not minding your own business is the direct result of not having business of your own to mind, and it is usually the fruit of idleness. Is it not interesting that when you are interfering with someone else they tell you to go back to your own work: "Mind your own business." A Christian's prime concern should not be with how everybody else is doing their job. His prime concern should not be how everybody else is behaving. His prime concern should be, "How am I getting on? How am I behaving?" A holy person is primarily concerned with their own business. The world would be a sweeter place if there were more holy people in it.

The third and last thing Paul mentions here is to work hard with your own hands. In Greek society people despised those who worked with their hands, they looked up to those who worked with their heads. Because the Greek outlook has influenced our society so deeply, we still think this way. We still think that someone who works with his hands is below in the social scale a man who works with his head. We talk about the white-collar workers as somehow a step up. Don't you believe it – that is man's way of judging people, not God's. When God sent his Son to earth he gave him a job with his hands – a carpenter for eighteen years. Paul himself, who was writing, was a tent maker even though he had been to university. He was not afraid of hard work.

I think there has been a whole lot of nonsense gathered around the phrase "living by faith". Paul lived by faith and he earned his living tent making. To reserve this phrase for those and only those who live on the gifts of others is just not a scriptural use of it. Paul says, "The life I now live I live by faith in the Son of God."

The normal pattern for every Christian is to support himself if he possibly can. It is a shameful thing for a Christian not to support himself if he could do so. Now the church has had a deep concern and compassion for those who could not support themselves. It has a record second to none (as you will know if you have studied church history) for looking after orphans, widows and the aged who could not support themselves. When the Barbarians invaded Milan a little over 1,400 years ago, they stormed into Milan Cathedral and said to the bishop, "Where are the treasures of the church?" They were going to take them back as loot. The bishop pointed to a door and he said, "We keep our treasures in there." When they opened the door, inside was a room full of orphans being given some soup. The church has always cared for those who could not support themselves, but there ought to be a self-respecting pride in a Christian that is prepared to take support from those who are served.

That applies whether you are a butcher or a preacher. A preacher or pastor is no different from any other employment according to the Bible – a labourer is worthy of his hire. If I for one moment felt that you were not getting your money's worth from me, I would immediately feel I was living on charity. Paul puts preaching – those who live by the gospel, benefitting others spiritually and receiving in return material support – on the same level as any other labourer. Paul came to Greek society where slaves were kept to do the work, that their owners might not dirty their hands, and that people might have leisure in order to be whatever they wished to be. In that society Paul says, "You know that I made tents. I didn't live on you, I made tents."

A Christian, if they possibly can, should make it their ambition, as Paul says, to be dependent on nobody. The implications of that need to be very thoroughly thought through, but they are real. Holiness consists in supporting yourself. In 2 Thessalonians he even goes so far as to say that if a man who could work will not work then he should not be given food even by Christians. Holiness consists in diligence and supporting yourself if you can – in not living on charity. But Christians who become unable to work and support themselves should surrender any pride and ask for the grace to receive—that also is a holy attitude.

So here we have been looking at holiness, sanctification. Do those words seem up in the clouds? Do they seem up in heaven? They are not, they are words right down here in this dirty old earth. This is where God has called us, not to uncleanness but to holiness in our relationships between men and women, in our relationships with our fellow believers, in our relationships with the people we work alongside; people who see us in our jobs. Why should we be holy like this? The teaching of Paul tells us: that you may earn the respect of those who never see you in church, those who do not hear you pray – that they may see the only part of your Christianity that they can see and say, "That's something real."

Too many Christians see the pursuit of holiness as a leisure time activity, something to do outside their working hours. May I plead with you: never think that your hours at work are cutting you off from the Christian life and the possibility of holiness. They are providing you with the very opportunity of holiness. Until we see this we are going to waste most of the hours of our waking life. So holiness is something right there, it is not a Sunday pursuit, it is a Monday morning pursuit. It is not a heavenly thing but an earthly thing. It was here that our Lord lived a holy life.

There is a glorious motive for holiness – v. 16 of this chapter is the noisiest verse in the Bible. There is a trumpet blasting, an archangel shouting, a noise enough to wake the dead – and that is precisely what happens. The rest of the chapter is about the second coming of our Lord Jesus Christ. It is called the royal visit of Jesus (the Greek word *parousia*, means "royal visit"). Here is the biggest motive for practical holiness there is in the Bible.

Once I stood in the House of Lords, just between the woolsacks and the royal throne, and looked at that magnificent setting where the Queen's Speech is given. I looked at the wrought brass rail around the throne, polished so you could see your face in it. I looked at the throne, covered with a dust sheet, to be removed when the Queen comes. It struck me then that, for a royal visit, everything must be spotless. If the Queen were coming to your house you would have the vacuum cleaner out, you would be dusting, polishing, shoving everything into cupboards, until it was fit for the royal visit.

Standing near the royal throne, I looked up because the man who was telling us various facts about it said, "You see this throne, it's carved of solid oak, it's the most marvellous piece of carving." I looked up just above the Queen's head and there was a spotlight just happening to catch the very ornate carving above, and I saw cobwebs and thick dust right above her head. She could have had a spider or a cobweb on her head. The Queen's throne – they had got most of it clean, but they had not got all of it clean. It just hit me: "Fancy the Queen sitting under that!"

There is a royal visit coming, and the King of kings, the Lord of lords, is coming right back to this planet. Paul is saying to the Thessalonians: I look at your faith, and that is ready for the King; I look at your hope – that is ready; I look at your love – well, that is nearly ready although you need a bit more of that. But I can see some cobwebs. I can see a lack of wholeness, I can see the gaps and the dirt. God is calling you to that holiness without which no-one will see the Lord. God is calling you to get everything clean for the King who is coming.

God wants us clean from end to end, ready for the King. Let us ask the Lord to show us where the cobwebs are in us.

5

Read 1 Thessalonians 4:13 – 5:11

A. THE DEAD AT HIS COMING (4:13–18)

1. Return of those who are asleep (13–14)
   a. Unwitting ignorance
   b. Unnecessary grief

2. Rapture of those who are alive (15–18)
   a. Dead elevated first
   b. Live elevated second

B. THE DATE OF HIS COMING (5:1–11)

1. Astonishment for those who are sleepy (1–3)
   a. Thief in the night
   b. Pains in pregnancy

2. Anticipation for those who are awake (4–11)
   a. Alert and controlled
   b. Armoured and protected

The next great world event in history will be the return of our Lord Jesus Christ to this planet earth. There are over three hundred references in the New Testament to this event and it is the very centre of the Christian's hope. It is the anchor within the veil to the Christian, the thing we cling to. Whatever damaging news and disturbing events there are around us, the Christian says: I am absolutely certain of one thing – my Jesus is coming back. It is a theme that is fundamental to Christian thinking. You cannot really preach the gospel adequately if you leave this out.

True, the gospel centres in what happened two thousand years ago when Jesus died on a cross. But then it is interesting that there are a similar number of references in the New Testament to the cross as to this event – his return to earth. Therefore we stand poised between these two events. No other event has as many references as these two. They are of equal importance to the Christian. Our faith looks back to the cross, our hope looks forward to his coming, and we live in between those two events.

The Bible does not answer all our questions about the second coming of Christ to this planet. Don't believe those who seem to have all the answers! Even if you try to work it out with charts and diagrams, you will still have to revise them each time you study your New Testament. We know some of the events that are going to occur, and some of the information that we are given is fascinating.

When Paul went to Thessalonica he preached the whole gospel, so from the very beginning he told his converts that Christ was coming back. So excited was Paul about this, so did he hope that it would happen in his own lifetime, that they got the message loud and clear – only too loud and only too clear, and they went a bit overboard on the second coming. The message they got was this: he may be coming back within our lifetime. Of course, every generation of

Christians hopes that. Part of my hope is that you will never see David Pawson's funeral announced. That is part of my hope because if Jesus comes back before I die then I will not die.

Because they grasped this part of what Paul was teaching them so firmly, and were so excited about it, they were terribly shaken when some of the church members died. The tragic thing is that the impression death leaves on us is that the person who has died is now out of everything and is going to miss it. You can feel that when you have buried the remains of a loved one or attended a crematorium service. There is a horrible feeling that they are out of things now and are going to miss everything we do now. They can no longer share in it. This was worrying the Thessalonian Christians very deeply.

They would have said: Paul some of our members have died since you were here, they are going to miss the coming of the Lord.

It is the kind of thought that comes to minds which have heard about the second coming. The sort of question we want to ask is: how does it affect us? How will it affect our loved ones? This was a natural reaction. Paul wrote to them in this letter and gave them some tremendous news which must have cleared up the doubt. He let the Thessalonians know that those believers who had died were going to get front seats. The dead in Christ will meet him first, and then we who are still alive will catch them up. It is a tremendous answer. Those who have died in Christ are not going to miss anything, they will get the first chance to see Jesus when he comes. That takes all their fear away, doesn't it?

So that takes the sting out of death. It would be lovely to go straight to the Lord Jesus during our lifetime and not have to go through the process of dying. But that may not be our portion. It was not Paul's. He hoped it would be but it wasn't.

A Christian is torn so many different ways. We want to be in this body, we want to go straight into the new body, we want to be around on earth when Jesus comes back, and yet on the other hand there is something in us that says, "No, I'd rather be off and depart and be with Christ. It's so much better." If you could see a single Christian from your church who is now dead and with the Lord in glory, you would envy their position. You would not want them to be back, you would want to change places with them. If we have blessings here, there is nothing that compares to being with the Lord. It is far better than everything we know here.

A Christian is not allowed the luxury of worldly grief at a time of bereavement. We are told that we are not to grieve, as others do who have no hope. How miserable the world is! You can tell a Christian funeral every time. There may be tears—yes, that's natural. The Lord wept at the tomb of Lazarus. There will be tears, but how unnatural it is.

I interviewed an undertaker and asked him, "What is the difference between Christian homes and others where there has been bereavement?"

I remember how he paused and thought, and then said, "Yes there is one difference I've noticed again and again. Something that is only true of Christian homes. I have never found resentment or bitterness in a Christian home, however tragic the circumstances of the death. I've found that in many other homes, but never in a Christian home."

That was a tribute, something unmistakable. We grieve but we do not grieve as others do who have no hope. It is not a hopeless despair – not the end. Why is death the great unmentionable? Why is it almost a dirty word now? You mustn't talk about it. If you bring it up in society you will be looked at askance. Why? – Because we live in a world that is without God and without hope. One Scottish professor has collected together some of the statements about death in the Greek world and the Roman world to which Paul was writing this letter. Here are some of the statements by great Greek thinkers. There was a man called Aeschylus who said, "Once a man dies, there is no resurrection." And Theocritus said, "There is hope for those who are alive but those who have died are without hope." That has come down to us in the modern proverb, "While there's life there's hope." Then there was Catullus, who said, "When once our brief life sets, there is one perpetual night through which we must sleep."

Here is a letter of sympathy sent to a bereaved person two thousand years ago: "Against such things as death one can do nothing, therefore comfort one another." Finally, here is one of the grimmest epitaphs on a tombstone there ever was. It is on a Greek tombstone not far from Thessalonica and it says underneath the name: "I was not, I became, I am not, I care not." That is the world's "hope" and that is why death is the unmentionable.

We are not to grieve as those who have no hope. We are not overcome with despair. True, we feel the parting, but if we grieve it is for ourselves, not for the dead person. They are not missing anything; they are far better off. We have lost someone precious to us for a time but it is not with that despair of never meeting that person again. One of the loveliest things in this little passage is this: When the Lord comes, he will bring back to us those whom we have lost in Christ. He will *bring* – isn't that a lovely word? You see, death for the world comes as a thief in the night, a robber that comes to take, but death for us will bring; the Lord will bring with him so many.

So let us look at what is going to happen to the dead at his coming. First of all, notice that for death Paul uses a phrase "fallen asleep". Think about the implications of this. You often see it on a gravestone. I saw inscribed on a gravestone: "Fallen asleep in Jesus." *In Jesus*—that, of course, makes all the difference. What is your address when you die? It is a wonderfully safe place to be – *in* Jesus. Have you ever wondered what it feels like actually to die? How you will feel in the moment of dying? I can tell you, very simply: you experience it every night, and it will be exactly the same as you experience every night of your life. You practise death every night. Did you know that? As far as your body is concerned, as far as this life is concerned, it is as simple as falling asleep. In a sense, you die every night. It may be a thought to you when you go to bed tonight. Just practise dying and say: "Lord, I'm dropping off now and if I wake up tomorrow morning with you then that would be great. But I am just going off to sleep right now and if I wake up in your presence, hallelujah."

I think of a dear lady who came to live at our home for the elderly. She was not a Christian and had no church connection as far as we knew, but we felt drawn to her and that we should take her into the home. She came in her early nineties. Her only claim to fame was that she was Britain's champion rifle shot. She had been a real athlete and in her carpet slippers she would run around the outside of the house every morning – a wonderful character.

After a bit she began to get interested in Christian things. She sensed Christian love in the home around her. She started reading her Bible at ninety-two. She came to the Lord and one day she called me into her little bedroom and she said, "Could I be baptised?" I said, "Most certainly," and we fixed the date. One night, just about a week later, while she was still very fit, she went to bed, went to sleep, and woke up in heaven. What a lovely way to go. It was as easy as that.

Those who have fallen asleep may have had some pain and weariness. There may have been a bit of a valley of a shadow before, but the moment of dying is like falling asleep. I think that comforts us. You have done it every night so it is just doing it once more. The only difference is that you wake up in a different place. The person you see will not be your wife, your husband or your family. You will see Jesus. Now some people have wrongly taken this phrase "fallen asleep", which simply describes the act or the event of death, and used it to teach that we shall be unconscious from that moment right through to the Lord's return, which could be many centuries later. I do not believe that you can read that into the scripture. I cannot believe that a man as alive as Paul, so full of energy, vigour, thought, life, prayer, praise and service would say, "an unconscious state is far better"!

Indeed we are going to see in chapter 5 that that is denied: "Whether we wake or sleep we live with him..." and being asleep is not what I call living. No, it is a conscious relationship. But from this side of death and in the immediate experience it is just falling asleep with the glorious certainty that you are going to wake up in the presence of the Lord. Why is it that you are not afraid to go to sleep at night? Why aren't you afraid to put your head on that pillow and shut your eyes and lose consciousness? It is because you go to sleep in the certainty in your heart: "I'll wake up tomorrow morning, make a cup of tea, and get on with the day's work." But once you have grasped that when you go to that final point of dropping off to sleep – if you are sure that you are going to wake up in the presence of Jesus, all fear goes. I want to assure you of that, and every minister has been at bedsides of people who have reached that point. I want to assure you that those who know they are just going to wake up with Jesus do not mind going to sleep. It is really as simple as that, or ought to be. There is a hymn:

Teach me to live that I may dread
The grave as little as my bed.
Teach me to die that so I may
Rise glorious on the judgment day.

That is a prayer that we need to pray – for Christianity not only teaches you how to live but it teaches you how to die too. You see, if you are in Jesus then what happens to Jesus happens to you. He died, but when he died he committed his Spirit to the Father and he rose again. We know that he was conscious and active even before he was reunited with his body during that period of three days and three nights. He was preaching, serving his Father. He was preaching to those who were drowned in Noah's day – the Bible tells us that quite simply. But then, at the resurrection, when his body was reunited with his Spirit, he was whole again. But he was active in between, and there are the events for the Christian. We will die, as Jesus died. We will have a fully conscious relationship with him immediately afterwards. Aren't you looking forward to the first five minutes after death? Then our new bodies will be given to us at his coming. We shall get those new bodies if we are dead – or, rather, if we are living with him while we sleep. Words lose their meaning, don't they? But if we are among those who are called the "dead" at that point, we will have that new body first and the living will have to catch up with us. We will see Jesus before they do – that is the teaching of scripture.

So with v. 16 we come to what has been described as the noisiest verse in the Bible. I do not know where people get the idea of a secret rapture – with trumpets blowing and archangels shouting and the Lord himself summoning the dead! People say nobody will notice. Don't you believe it – it is enough to wake the dead, and it will.

I remember going to see the work of an artist, Stanley Spencer, who painted a marvellous picture of a Thames village church with the tombs and graves around it. The stones are pushed aside and people are coming out of their graves all over the churchyard, and instead of being a dead area, the whole place is crawling with life. It is a tremendous picture. Some people find it a bit grotesque but I found it exciting.

Spirits have been alive and conscious all that interval, but one day the bodies wake up again – that is the resurrection. Whole people are made new. So they get there first, then in a moment, in a twinkling of an eye, those of us who are alive shall be changed. They call us the "quick", but believe me the dead will be quicker. They will be there, we who are alive will catch them up, and then comes the biggest meeting of Christians there has ever been. No stadium on earth could hold them. So we will just have to be up in the air in a three-dimensional meeting. Meeting with the Lord up in the air – how significant: Satan is called in the Bible the prince of the power of the air but in that day the air will belong to the Christians.

I suppose the first sign that some people will get of it will be the sign that our Lord told us, and it is a pretty frightening one. There will be two in one kitchen, and suddenly one will be alone. Two in one bed, husband and wife, and suddenly the partner has gone. It is not right to frighten one another with panic into the kingdom. You must come to the Lord because you want your sins dealt with. But many people have been awakened in conscience by the thought that families will be split, friends will be separated and relatives will be parted. Now it may be the first thing that people know of what is happening: that the Christians have gone to meet the Lord – disappeared.

I have often looked at the words engraved (at his request) on my grandfather's tombstone in Newcastle: "What a meeting!" What a thing to put on a gravestone! There must be many who pass that grave, right on the main path in the cemetery who must look at it and think: "What kind of odd person is buried there?" But I know that my grandfather, my father and my great-grandfather will be at that meeting, not because we are related to each other but because they fell asleep in Christ. So there is to be a reunion.

The glorious thing is that we shall be with *him* and with *his* – not just with him forever but with *his*, for he will bring with him those who are looking forward to meeting again. "So comfort one another with these words." People say that only words cannot bring comfort. No, they cannot if it is just words, and how often we are tongue-tied when someone is bereaved. We want to comfort them but we do not know quite how to speak. We are more comfortable writing letters so that we can spend a long time thinking of the next sentence. We try to comfort one another with words, and when you hear worldly people trying to comfort each other after death, isn't it pathetic and sad? "Well, he didn't suffer long...." All kinds of words are used.

Paul is telling the believers to comfort one another with words which are the Word of the Lord. If it is *his* word then you have got *his* word for it and you can comfort one another with them – not with human words but with divine words, the word of the Lord that he will bring with him those who have fallen asleep in him. There is not a word here about those who have fallen asleep *outside* Christ. The Bible is very reticent, even silent on the state of those who have died outside Christ. There are just one or two hints and they are pretty frightening, one of which is in Luke 16, the parable of the rich man and the beggar at his gate. People keep asking what will happen to those outside of Christ You are telling them the good news of what happens to those who fall asleep in Jesus. They ask because they are anxious to find a tolerable alternative. They want some comfort that they are going to be all right outside of Christ and you cannot give it. That is why everything in me rebels when I am asked to take a funeral of someone who has died outside of Christ. I do not know what to say. If I tell the truth, I will just put the relatives in more distress. You see, the Bible says very little about that side. If we have heard about Christ, our only question should be: "Am I going to fall asleep in Christ?" not: "What's going to happen to those who fall asleep outside of Christ?" If I am desperately anxious to know about them, it rather reveals to me that it is not that I have a concern for *them*, it is that I might be among them and I just want to be sure I am going to be alright – that there will be a second chance; that somehow it is not so bad. But the Bible tells us that those who fall asleep in Jesus have all this to look forward to. That is enough. Make sure you fall asleep in him.

Now let us move from the first question of the dead at his coming to the date of his coming, which is always a question that has intrigued us: *when*? If you will just tell me the date I will get ready. Can you see now why he does not tell us? If I knew the date it would either be so near that I would run around in little circles panicking; or, if it was not near, I would say, "Fine I can get on with my business. I can enjoy myself. I've got another however many years." So God in his wisdom says, "As to the times and seasons". People have made the mistake of trying to date the second coming. Martin Luther did, John Wesley did; many of the great preachers have done. It is one of the easiest things in the world to drop into this. In the twentieth century, many times I used to be asked, "Do you think it will be before the year two thousand?"

I will not pin myself down as to the times and seasons. When Christ comes back it will be the most terrible shock to the world. It will be like a burglar coming, and when a burglar comes you do not expect it. If you had, you would have been up, watching. You would have had the dog on his chain outside. You would have been ready.

Sudden destruction, so unexpected, like a pregnant woman who suddenly clutches her stomach and the pains have

83

started. Once they have started there is no escape, it has got to go through. Here is Paul's vivid picture. Jesus used the same expression "Like a thief in the night". Here is the important thing: does the church go through the tribulation or not? One of the things that seems to me to indicate that this will not be a sudden "any moment" thing but something for which watchful Christians will be fully ready and aware is precisely Paul's word: "You will not be surprised." It is not like a thief in the night to Christians, but only to those who are asleep. Now here is the second use of the word "asleep" in a totally different sense. Now he is not using it of those who have died in Christ but of those who are living outside of Christ. They are the ones really asleep. In fact until you know Christ, you are asleep. You may not think it but you are. Philosophers have been teasing their heads for centuries over the question "How do you know the difference between being awake and being asleep?" In an Oxford examination in philosophy, one of the leading questions was: "How do you know you are not dreaming?" The students had to give reasons why they thought they were not dreaming as they wrote the exam paper. How do you know you are not dreaming at this moment? How do you know you are awake and not asleep? It is an intriguing question. You might just be dreaming it all up. I certainly have dreams about taking services in which everything goes wrong. I have left my notes at home and I have picked the wrong hymn and the hymn book is printed upside down – and I am dreaming. But I have had some experiences like that while awake and it has been a "nightmare"! It is interesting that we use that term for a difficult experience.

According to the Bible, until you are Christian you are dreaming. You are asleep. You are living in a world of dream and delusion. You are not connecting up with reality at all. In fact, that is the most dangerous "sleep". That is why the

Bible says, "Awake you that sleep. Let Christ's light shine upon you. Awake. Rise from the dead, awake – you are asleep." What is the sign of a person who is asleep? They may be having thoughts and experiences. They may see faces, they may dream all kinds of things but they are not in touch with reality. A person who is not a Christian is not in touch with reality but thinks that the things that you handle and touch and see are reality. But it is the unseen things that are eternal. A person who has not woken up yet in Christ is just not in touch. They are living in an illusion that this world is here forever, an illusion that material things satisfy, a dream world. It happens to the drug addict, it happens to the alcoholic. They get to the point where they do not know whether they are real or not real, awake or asleep, they cannot distinguish reality.

So Paul says that we are of the day not of the night. We are awake, not asleep. We are sober not drunk. We are destined for salvation not destruction. What a contrast he draws. There is a very real emphasis in connection with the second coming on being *sober*. I take it quite literally that it means that. He is talking about getting drunk. Far more people get drunk in the darkness than do in the light. Can you imagine anything worse for a Christian than to be the worse for drink when he meets Christ? Be sober; be sober in full possession of yourself, alert, awake, and on guard. You are on sentry duty. The Christian sentry is put there to watch and to pray.

I heard a very amusing story of an army sentry on duty in a sentry box and he was leaning against the side of it. It was the early hours of the morning and he just dropped off like that. He suddenly heard the sergeant, "Hmmmph!" He jumped up and the sergeant said, "What are you doing – sleeping?" He replied, "No, just saying my prayers." That was quick and he certainly got out of a nasty situation. But let us put those two together: a sentry watches and prays. He must be on guard. We are living in hostile, dangerous days, and if we are going to be ready for the Lord's return we need to be on guard, armoured. To keep your head these days you must have the helmet of hope, and to keep your heart intact you must have faith and love.

As a sentry watching and praying, waiting for the Lord's return, you will be ready and you will not be caught by a surprise. You will know when it is coming. There will be no surprise to Christians. Said Jesus again and again: watch and pray; when you see these things begin to happen, lift up your heads, your redemption draws near. In 2 Thessalonians 2 we will see that Paul writes to these very Christians saying: what are you getting so excited about the second coming for? You are panicking; you have left your jobs. Go back to work. There are certain things that must happen before Christ comes, it will not be in "any moment." Based on my reading of scripture I do not believe that it could happen tonight, because there are certain things that Paul describes which have got to happen first and have not yet happened, though with the speed of world events they could happen very quickly.

But I would not be true to the Bible that I preach and seek to understand if I said, "Now you get to Christ tonight or you might not be here in the morning." What I can say is that, with the speed of world events and the changes that are happening, it could be much nearer than you think. Be ready now, be ready all the time: with helmet of hope, breastplate of faith and love, head and heart intact, sober, alert, disciplined, watching, praying, serving the Lord; and, hallelujah, behold the bridegroom comes, and those whose lamps are burning go in with him. They are ready, watching and waiting.

"Therefore brethren," says Paul, "encourage one another and build each other up." One of the biggest mistakes we make in the Christian life is that we take the words of God, the words of scripture, the words of the Lord, and we try to comfort *ourselves* with them. But, notice carefully, again and again Paul doesn't say comfort *yourself* with these thoughts and with these words, but comfort *one another*. Don't try to pick yourself up. Minister to someone else the Word of the Lord and let them minister to you. Share these things and build each other up just as you are doing.

6

Read 1 Thessalonians 5:12 – 28

A. TO YOUR ELDERS (12–13a)
1. Respect   2. Love

B. TO EACH OTHER (13b–15)
1. Do – warn idle, encourage timid, help weak
2. Don't – take revenge

C. TO YOURSELVES (16–18)
1. Rejoice always   2. Pray continually
3. Thank in all circumstances

D. TO HOLY SPIRIT ((19–22)
1. Despise nothing   2. Test everything
3. Keep good

E. TO GOD (23–24)
1. Sanctify you thoroughly
2. Blameless at his coming
3. Faithful to do it

FINAL EXHORTATIONS
1. Mutual intercession
2. Physical affection
3. Total attention

In the Bible the Word of God is described as a two-edged sword, but I think if you updated that and paraphrased it for today, you would say the Word of God is like an armour-piercing shell. It gets right through your defences. If it is an armour-piercing shell, then I would say this passage at the end of 1 Thessalonians 5 is like a machine gun — the bullets just fly. There are about thirty of them altogether in the last few verses of chapter 5, and they penetrate very deeply but they come so much on top of one another that you feel battered at the end. He suddenly seems to speed up and with staccato, telegraphic phrases he fires these words out one after another on all kinds of subjects.

Each one of them is a real pearl of wisdom, but before we look at them bit by bit let us ask whether there is a string running through the pearls, or are they just like a lot of pearls running around with a snapped necklace? I think there is a "string" – one theme that runs all the way through: relationships. Every bit of advice he gives us here is concerned with your relationships – with your elders, your fellow members, your circumstances; and your relationship to the Holy Spirit, your relationship to yourself, and then back again, because it is so important, to your relationship to your brethren. We are going to look at these.

Now I want you to notice that though I have said "advice" they are much more than good advice. Paul says, "I beseech you, I exhort you, I command you, I warn you", which are very strong words. These are commands; these are the marching orders for the Christian. A Christian has no choice whatever as to whether to do these things or not. They are presented to us with one phrase right in the middle of them: "For this is the will of God." If you are a Christian, you are here to do God's will, not here to do your own will. You are not here to do other people's will, you are here to do God's will. Therefore, as we read these things, we are not reading good advice on how to keep the church happy. This is the will of God—this is the pattern of relationships which he commands – and it will be for our good, of course.

A church that does these things will be a happy, fruitful church. It will be a lovely church to be in, but that is not why we are given these commands, it is because it is the will of God. Of course, if you do his will there is always blessing, but we do it first because it is his will. We would do it, I hope, even if there was no blessing attached to it, though thank God there is. Having pointed that out, let me give you one other word of introduction. Satan is determined to destroy the church. It is the one instrument of God in this world that is undoing his work and so he is against the church. There are two favourite devices he has for the individual Christians. One is to keep them out of membership of a local church. If he can do that, he can prevent them from ever obeying this passage. If he can keep you out of the fellowship of a local church, and keep you in the relationship of a permanent visitor of that church, he will do so because then you do not need to respect those who are over you in the Lord because there are no Christians over you in the Lord. You can lord it over yourself and that is a dangerous position to be in. Every Christian needs the protection of eldership. The second thing that Satan does if he cannot keep you out of membership is that he will put you in membership but divide you off from the other members. It is an old tactic, a well-known device: divide the opposing forces and they are too weak to attack you. So if the devil cannot keep you out of membership of a church, he may put you right into it and so use you that in fact you break up that church rather than build it up.

That is the background, and although Satan is not mentioned in this passage, everything is commanded against Satan. One other thing before we go into it: this passage is profoundly unnatural. A Christian is not someone who, to quote what was a pop song when I was a teenager, is: "Doing what comes naturally". A Christian is the very opposite of that, for every one of these commands is telling you not to do what comes naturally but to do what comes supernaturally, and that is a much more difficult thing, cutting right across human nature.

When Paul went to Thessalonica, it was said of him and his helpers: "These who turn the world upside down have come here too." In fact this passage turns the Christian upside down and it tells you to do the very opposite of what you would do by nature.

We are told about our relationship to our elders of our local church (because there are no other elders in scripture except elders of local churches): "But we beseech you brethren to respect those who labour among you and are over you in the Lord and admonish you, and to esteem them very highly in love because of their work."

One of the greatest differences between denominations is the way they approach the question of church government. This is perhaps something that is holding us apart in England. There are Christians who love the Bible, who are born again of the Spirit, and who know the Lord, but are wedded to different patterns of church government, and these patterns override the things we have in common. It is a sad situation and it behoves us all to go back to the Bible and ask what kind of government the Bible intends us to have.

If the Bible intends us to have popes then let us get under a pope and be united. If the Bible intends us to have bishops then let us get under a bishop and be united. But let us look at what it does say. Let me say that the typical Baptist pattern of church government is not to be found within scripture either, nor is the Brethren pattern to be found. Of one church in which I ministered I would have said we were "orthodox, catholic, pentecostal, baptist, congregational, brethren" –

every one of those words intentionally spelt with a lower case initial letter!

I am going to approach this matter not from the point of view of any other denomination but from the point of view of Baptist churches. If I caricature, forgive me but I am trying to present what can occur and which is not scriptural. The church was never intended to be a dictatorship of one man or a democracy in which all the members try to run the show. Many Baptist churches have found themselves torn between the minister trying to do his will and all the members in the church meeting trying to do theirs. It either finishes up with the minister becoming such a dictator that the church begins to dwindle and members leave it, or the members so controlling the minister that he finishes up in some other occupation. I have seen that happen in church after church after church, and the reason of course was that neither position was the scriptural one. The scriptural one is the pattern of joint leadership. No man should be the sole leader of a church nor should every member try to be the leader. God's pattern is the best and the wisest: that there should be recognised within every fellowship those whom God has called and equipped and given to the fellowship to be its joint leaders. So that no one man can have the monopoly of leadership, and so that the members may not have the monopoly of leadership, but that wise leadership may be exercised. That is God's pattern – a plurality of men to lead the family. You can call them "bishops" if you like. Some translations of the New Testament do, and I do not object to the word.

In discussion, a member of another denomination asked me, "Do you believe in bishops?" I replied, "Yes, we have quite a few of them," and he looked so surprised. I said, "Yes, we've got six or seven of them already and we are hoping for more." It is just a name. But some translations use the word bishop or overseer, foreman or elder—they are all translations of the Greek meaning these men. But it is a shared leadership that is referred to. When we had a baptismal service in the church I mentioned earlier, you never saw one man baptising. It is the church that is baptising – a shared responsibility, and whether someone would be baptised or not became a decision shared by the elders. In fact, church membership was taken further – to the whole church.

So shared decisions and shared leadership was the pattern of the church in the New Testament. You can have the leaders that God has given and you can receive them and recognise them, but the vital thing is whether you continue to respect them afterwards. No leaders can operate if they do not have the respect of those they seek to lead. That respect is not due to their personality, it is not due to anything they wear, that respect is due to one thing only: the work they seek to do. Anarchy and chaos result from the loss of respect for the work that a man has been given to do.

One of the most difficult things an elder has to learn to do – and it is hard to give and even harder to receive – is admonition. It is part of an elder's task to admonish those who are, as the Bible says, "playing truant" in some way, those who are not pulling their weight, not fulfilling their duties.

I have noticed that elders take some time to learn how to be firm in this regard. But that is one of the reasons why the choice of an elder should depend on his children, his family. If he cannot discipline his own children or be firm with them when they do wrong, and admonish them wisely, he will not make a good elder in the family of God. This, then, is one of the tests. It is an acid test, but it is there and it is even harder to receive admonition and love the person you received it from. But the Bible says respect them. Not for their temperament or personality, not for any status, simply because of the work they have been called to do. If they admonish you, love them for it. Do not jump to the conclusion they admonish you because they enjoy admonishing people. They do it for the family's sake and in love.

That is the first thing that is needed in a church that is going to tackle Satan, and which is really going to march into battle – because an army that does not recognise any leadership will get absolutely nowhere in the field. The church is like a mighty army and it should overcome the hosts of Satan. It is the host of God, and therefore leadership is a key to it, but respect for that leadership is vital.

The Word says that he *labours* among you. That word means it is tough, it is hard. I do not think you would be willing to swap your place in the church with that of an elder if you knew all that they are called upon to do, the burdens they are called upon to carry, the calls they have to make, the problems they have to try and untangle, the guidance they have to try to give, knowing that all the time they must watch over the flock as those who must give account, and they are those to whom the Lord will say, "Now how did you lead my flock?"

That is the first relationship mentioned here. Let us now look at the second: the relationship with your fellow Christian. "Be at peace among yourselves and we exhort you brethren: admonish the idle, encourage the fainthearted, help the weak, be patient with them all, see that none of you repays evil for evil but always seek to do good to one another and to all."

We have elders to whom we give respect as they labour among us as leaders of the fellowship. But the next danger is that the members then think, "Fine, we have got elders, we can leave all the job to them; it is now their responsibility to encourage the fainthearted and support the weak." It is great to have elders, and if we have more problems than they can cope with let a church have some more elders. But listen to this word addressed to all the Christians at Thessalonica. It is your job also to be looking after one another, to be concerned with one another. Be at peace with one another; create harmony with one another, be together.

I love the word *together*, it comes right through the New Testament. How are you going to get that kind of peace? Not by limiting your contact with people to a handshake and a "Good morning" and a "Good evening". You can have a relative peace like that but it is not real peace. Peace comes when people are together in harmony and not just, as one man put it to me, I thought pretty crudely but very realistically: "I extend to people a hand of fellowship and keep them at arm's length. Then I can keep in peace." That is not peace, it is not close enough. You are not really at peace with one another until you have come close enough to hurt one another and let that heal.

So the very next verse says, "Admonish the idle, encourage the fainthearted, and help the weak." Members of the church do that, not just the elders. Watch over one another. You have got the difficult task of admonition. If you see a fellow Christian who is not pulling his weight, the word is literally, as I have said "playing truant", as for a soldier who goes AWOL (the term used for being "absent without leave" in the forces) and this is the literal word used here. Christians have a duty to watch over fellow Christians and if anyone goes absent without leave admonish them, tell them: you are not pulling your weight. "Encourage the fainthearted" is almost the opposite of that one. It means somebody who is scared stiff, somebody who is over cautious, somebody who is so frightened in any meeting that they look around for the most inconspicuous seat and make for it. To encourage the fainthearted means to look out for the timid.

It is a bit shattering to discover that there are people who can come to your church literally for years and still say they do not feel they know anybody in the fellowship. If you see somebody who is scared to join in a prayer meeting and pray out loud, sit alongside of them and say, "Look just give a little sentence and I'll pray along while you do" – that is encouraging the fainthearted. If you know somebody who is scared stiff to go out and do a bit of house-to-house visiting with you, just say, "Look, I'll go with you. I'll do the first few. Then when you're ready to, you do it." Encourage the fainthearted and support the weak. That phrase "support the weak" is a revolution. It is not natural to support the weak. What is natural is what Charles Darwin discovered in nature—the survival of the fittest. Do thank God that you live in a Christianised country (I don't say a Christian country) but a Christianised country in which this principle "support the weak" has so spread through our society that people accept it as natural to look after the feeble and the weak. Many societies in the world do not do it.

I was reading a thrilling account of a revival that broke out in South West Africa after twelve years of missionary work. In one of the most primitive societies in Africa, two clan leaders announced that they wanted to be cleansed of their sinful existence and follow the Way. Do you know what the immediate result was? Age-old customs like the killing of twin babies stopped, and the neglect of feeble, old people stopped. Who says Christianity is not relevant? What happens in a society where there is no trace of Christianity? Well, the weak are not always supported, but in a redeemed community of Christian people the weak ought to have first consideration. We can do it, of course, quite easily in an affluent society. The test comes when we haven't enough for ourselves. The test comes when we are in the position of families we have heard about in Bangladesh and India where the father and mother deliberately had to decide which of their children to starve, and they had so little food that when they had a meal one child had to sit it out and did not have anything. Did they always choose the weakest child? No.

If you are going to go around trying to admonish the idle, encourage the fainthearted and support the weak, then you will need to be patient with them all, which is the next phrase. Not everybody appreciates admonition. Not every fainthearted person wants to be encouraged. Be patient with them all. When we are tempted to get impatient, as all of us are, remember how patient God was with us, how long-suffering he was with every one of us.

So that is relationship with each other. But there is something else important: "Never repay evil with evil." I remember a missionary in India telling some Indians about that phrase: do good to those who hate you or bless those who curse you, and return good for evil, and you will heap coals of fire on his head. Someone said, "Oh, I'd love to see coals of fire on his head, so I will return good for evil." But I remember another little phrase that somebody wrote: "To return evil for evil is beastlike; to return good for good is manlike; to return evil for good is Satan-like, but to return good for evil is Christ-like." Retaliation, revenge, should never have any place in Christian fellowship.

Now let us look at the next relationship – to our circumstances. "Rejoice always, pray constantly, give thanks in all circumstances for this is the will of God in Christ Jesus for you." Have you had a bad week? Or a good week? Or a middling week? The phrase "in all circumstances" applies to all those three kinds of week, not just one. "Rejoice always"; "Pray constantly"; "Give thanks". All three phrases are qualified by this phrase "in all circumstances". You cannot give thanks *for* all circumstances and fortunately, the Bible never tells us to, but it says *in* all circumstances rejoice, pray, give thanks. Learn to relate all circumstances to the Lord. In fact this is the secret of joy. It does not say take pleasure or be happy.

Have you met Christians who think you have got to be happy all the time? They are just as bad as those who think you have to be miserable all the time. In fact, the real command of scripture is to *rejoice all the time* and that is deeper than happiness. You can rejoice when you are unhappy, you can rejoice in prison. You can pray constantly. That does not mean pray regularly as if once you have had your regular "quiet time" you have finished. It really means pray all the time, not that you must be on your knees all the time nor that you must shut your eyes all the time. But meaning: all the time be referring things to the Lord. Whatever your circumstances, you can pray – he is there.

When my wife is around, I may constantly refer something to her. Because she is there I will just break into something. If something is bursting in my heart through preparation, as it often is, I want to go and tell her about it and say, "I've just found something tremendous in Thessalonians!" I burst in and share it immediately, I do not wait until we have a "quiet time" together later that night. We share it, and this is what "pray constantly" means. You have got a problem in the middle of the morning in the office, pray then; refer it then. You do not need to shut your eyes, nor even to speak out loud, but you can refer it straight away. In all your circumstances there are the three dimensions: rejoice, pray, give thanks. The third is the result of the other two. If you are rejoicing and you are praying, you will give thanks.

The classic case of this is in the story of that great Dutch Christian lady Corrie ten Boom. She was dragged off to a concentration camp as a Christian guilty of sheltering Jewish families and hiding them. She loved the Bible and so she loved the Jews, and her family did. When she got to that camp, they were put in the hut with the worst infestation of bed bugs and fleas in the whole camp. That hut was notorious. She thought: why do we have to come in here, why couldn't we get another hut? But then she describes how she remembered that in all circumstances she must rejoice and give thanks. So she and Betsie, her sister, prayed and they gave thanks to God for the fleas and the bed bugs. The sisters started a Bible study and prayer meeting, and women were coming from all the other huts to this meeting and learning about the Lord, and only months later did they ask why the German guards never came and disturbed their meetings. Why did they never stop the women praying and reading the Bible? The answer: the fleas and the bed bugs! Wasn't that wonderful? The very thing for which they had given thanks had enabled them to hold their meetings. The thing for which they praised God he used to enable them to perform a ministry in that place. One day, Betsie, who died in the camp, said, "Corrie, after the war is over, let's get a house in the country so that we may have some of these people to stay and show them love." Corrie replied, "Oh that's a wonderful idea. These poor prisoners who are going through this, it'll be just what they need after the war." Betsy said, "No I didn't mean the prisoners, I meant the guards."

Rejoice always, pray constantly, and give thanks in all circumstances – Corrie is the perfect example of someone who learned to do that. Then you are never under your circumstances, you are always on top of them. You are always in charge of life, life is never in charge of you. No matter what your circumstances, in all these things you are more than conquerors through him that loved you. That is your relationship to circumstances.

There is our relationship to the Holy Spirit, "Don't quench the Spirit. Don't despise prophesying but test everything. Hold fast what is good and abstain from every form of evil."

There are two extremes in fellowships today: there are those churches that will have nothing of what the Spirit is doing and there are those churches who will swallow anything, and somewhere in between is the right balance. When churches won't have anything of what the Spirit is doing, of course this is due to fear of anything spontaneous, excessive caution, fear of emotionalism. I am as keen as anyone not to have any emotional*ism* in church, but I want emotion in church. That is part of me and part of you. I am not just a computer with a brain. I am a heart that feels and if we can't feel in our religion then God help us. If we can't get excited about God's Word, if we can't feel deeply the love and the grace of our Lord Jesus, we must be made of stone.

One thing the Holy Spirit is wanting to do is bring freedom to God's people and bring more emotion to them so that they can feel God's love. He wants to scatter more gifts among his people and he wants more of his people to be ministering. One minister in a church is not enough for the Holy Spirit. He wants every member to be a minister. He wants to spread the gifts so that we minister to one another. So Paul says don't put the fire out; don't quench the Spirit. I know that zeal and enthusiasm can go overboard. As someone has said, when a fire first starts there is smoke and the smoke gets in your eyes, and the cure for that is to fan the flames and get it hotter, not to cool it down.

When the Holy Spirit burns, he burns with fire. Tongues of flame came on the early church. I have been in a meeting where that happened in this generation. The Holy Spirit comes like fire, but you can put a fire out. He does not force you to accept what he wants to give. You can quench the fire, dampen it down, saying, "No, it's all got to be very nice and ordered and dignified and quiet here." The Holy Spirit is like new wine in an old bottle and he wants to break out.

The trouble is that when fellowships get that freedom,

and when individual Christians find it, they so often go to the other extreme and they swallow anything. They go to the opposite extreme where they do not test things, where they do not discern, and where anything that sounds exciting and is sensational and comes in the name of the Spirit is swallowed. What a balance here. "Don't quench the Spirit" but on the other hand "test everything". The reason for testing it is not to go home and criticise it. The reason is so that you may hold fast what is good and just discard what is not.

We had chicken for lunch. We said our usual grace for chicken: "Thank you for the birds we eat," and then we ate. We separated the flesh from the bones and there was something left on everybody's plate that was no good for us – and that is what you are to do. Do not lose your critical faculties. Test everything; discern it. There are scriptural tests for prophecy that is not of God. If a man predicts something and it does not come true, don't listen. Look for the fruits. There are many tests. The gifts of the Spirit will always exalt Jesus. Just as we separated flesh from bone at our lunch, do separate good from bad. Never despise prophesying. I know it may not be as interesting or exciting as preaching sometimes, but prophesying is a very important gift of God. It is God's way of speaking directly to a congregation, and he may use the most unlikely person, but test it. Hold fast what is good – separate it out. You can leave behind what is not. "Flee from everything that looks like evil," says Paul, but, "hold on to what is good."

Next, we think about our relationship to ourselves: "May the God of peace himself sanctify you holy and may your spirit and soul and body be kept sound and blameless at the coming of our Lord Jesus Christ. He who calls you is faithful and he will do it." When I say "attitude to yourself", what do I mean? I mean that you are made up of various parts. You can see that a human body has different parts, and you are also made up of soul and spirit. Some people are rather puzzled by this – body, soul, and spirit, what is the difference? As far as I understand the Bible, the body is the physical part of you, the "outside" of you, the spirit is the inside part of you that relates to God, and the soul is the natural life in you that brings the two together and keeps them together.

It is interesting that the word "soul" is applied in the Bible to animals, but the word "spirit" never is. God breathed into the dust of the earth and Adam became a living soul, which means body and spirit were united and therefore he was a soul. In Genesis 1 it says that God made creeping creatures and all kinds of things living souls after their own kind. So an animal is a living soul, it just doesn't have a spirit. Soul means life: "You fool, this night your soul will be required...." Your life will be required. "What shall it profit a man if he gains the whole world and loses his soul?" Modern Bibles say, "What shall it profit a man if he gains the whole world and loses his life?" Well, it is not profit. It is dead loss because he would have to leave everything behind. Have you got the meaning of "soul"? That means your life, and it is your soul that pulls your body and spirit together. When your life ends, your body and spirit separate. When Jesus died, he didn't commend his soul to go up, but his spirit. His soul was going, his life was going, and his spirit he commended to God – and Joseph of Arimathea laid his body in the tomb. You are made up of these three things: your outside, your inside, and the life that is keeping them together.

Paul is saying: don't you want all of that to be God's? May the God of peace sanctify – the outside of you, the inside of you, the very life that holds the two together—all of you sanctified, made holy, set apart.

The last two verses of Zechariah 14 say something so wonderful. In the last vision of Jerusalem as it will be one day when Christ rules over it, Zechariah said, "The horse's bells had inscribed on them, 'Holy to the Lord' and the pots and the pans in every kitchen in Judah were, 'Holy to the Lord' and sacred as the bowls on the altar." Zechariah caught a vision in which sacred and secular were no longer divided, in which there was no division between what we do on Monday and what we do on Sunday. There were no holy places, or rather every place was holy. No holy objects, every object was holy because there were holy people. It is sinners who need holy things. In the Old Testament, which was written for Jews, sinners, they had a holy place and holy utensils, holy vestments, but in the New Testament, which is written for saints, there are no holy places, no holy vestments, only holy people. The result is that everything can be brought in.

I told the members of a church that its new building was erected on the assumption that it would be peopled by saints, so we did not have a holy place, and I do not wear holy clothes! That was why we could perform a play right there and why we could eat and drink there. We want the whole building to be holy. We want the whole neighbourhood to be holy. We want everything we do to be holy – whether music, dancing, drama, whatever. We want to bring it in and make it sacred to the Lord. You can either make everything secular as the world is doing, or, as the religious sinners try to do, you can have your religion all holy with holy language, holy buildings with archways all over them, and you can try and make it different and keep all the music you sing in church holy music that is different from other music. Or, as a saint of God, you can say, "I want to bring it all in. I want to bring in the taxis and the buses; I want to bring in the trains and planes. I want to bring the business and the computer. I want to bring it and offer it to God. I want it all to be holy." May the God of peace take you, body, soul, and spirit, whatever part of you there is, and may he sanctify you holy and set you apart holy because he is holy. It is not only a question of we *must* be holy because he is holy, it is that we *can* be holy because he is holy. He is faithful and he will do it. As you look at another believer, think that you are looking at someone who is going to be perfect. I look at other Christians and I see them in Christ as saints. Let that go right in. May the God of peace sanctify you holy – he will do it. He never leaves a job half finished and he never leaves the person half sanctified. So may the God of peace take all of you and may your relationship to yourself be such that every part of you is *in* him.

We go back now to the relationship with the *brethren*. That lovely word occurs five times here. "Pray for us." Here is the greatest missionary and apostle there has ever been and he is saying: will you pray for me? Do you pray for ministers in missions and those from whom you have received the word? They need it badly. Do you pray for one another? Pray for those on the list of members of your church. You might pray for two members each day. You are probably prayed for yourself, even if you do not realise it.

"Greet all the brethren with a holy kiss." What does it mean? Just this: simply *show* your affection. I sometimes wish I had not been born and bred in England. We are frightened stiff of touching each other. I know of men who touched their dogs more than their children. When you meet a man like that and see his children, you realise what the children have missed. It does not mean that we have to be legalistic about this but that we have to be natural about it, and what is natural for you is to show your affection for someone. After all we are a family, brothers and sisters. Of course, Paul puts in the word "holy", knowing that until we are entirely sanctified there is always the possibility that this can be misunderstood – that it even can be misleading. Do not be so scared of the dangers that you develop a phobia.

J.B. Phillips translates it: "Give a good warm handshake all round." Well, if that is the natural way for you to show your affection, do so, but be gentle (some people have a tremendously firm handshake!)

"I adjure you by the Lord that this letter be read to all the brethren." This was the first letter ever written to become part of our New Testament. When Paul wrote to the Thessalonians, he did not know that it would be part of the Bible. I am sure he did not realise that we would be reading it two thousand years later. He simply said, "Read it out in church," and we have been reading it out in church ever since and it is now part of the New Testament – apostolic writing.

Finally the secret of it all, the "how". When I began preaching, someone gave me a word of good advice: "David, never finish a sermon without telling the congregation *how*. It is not enough to tell people what we ought to do, tell us how to do it." I will tell you how: "the grace of our Lord Jesus be with us all" – that is how. You will not respect the elders until the grace of the Lord Jesus is in your heart. You won't be at peace with one another until the grace of the Lord Jesus is in your heart. You won't be able to rejoice and pray and give thanks in all circumstances unless the grace of the Lord Jesus is in your heart. You won't be able to be sanctified holy apart from the Lord Jesus. You cannot make yourself good. Have you ever tried standing in front of the mirror every morning and saying "I'm determined to be humbled." You try it – it can't be done. But the grace of the Lord Jesus, the undeserved love that he gives you, the forgiveness that he gives to you, the sheer unmerited favour of the Lord Jesus, the love in his heart for every one of you – let that love in. Let the grace of the Lord Jesus forgive your sins and make you a new creature and then you can begin to live like this. The grace of the Lord Jesus will make a family in which we are all brethren.

7

Read 2 Thessalonians 1

A. PAST (1–4)
1. Ultimate (1–2)
    a. Father and Son
    b. Grace and peace
2. Immediate (3–4)
    a. Thanksgiving to God
    b. Boasting in church

B. FUTURE (5–12)
1. Ultimate (5–10)
    a. Retribution for sinners
    b. Rest for sufferers
2. Immediate (11–12)
    a. Worthy and working
    b. Glory and grace

We have been studying the first letter to the Thessalonians and now we have come to the second one. I wonder if you see any significance in that? The *second* letter – then the first one did not work. There is a very profound message here: the Christian life is not one gigantic leap that puts everything right, it is a series of steps in the right direction. That is why it is often described as a walk. Sometimes it is described as running the race, sometimes it is described as a stand – that when you are under attack, having done all, you stand – but most frequently the Christian life is described as a walk. We are to walk worthy of our calling, to walk in light, to walk in love, to walk as children of the light.

Paul knew that one letter did not necessarily put all problems right or answer all questions. It needed following up because the first letter didn't do the trick. He did not write them off, he shared with them further thoughts. Paul might have had to write seventeen letters to the Thessalonians for all I know. It has been said that much good work is lost for lack of a little more. In other words, when you have done one thing for someone, there may be something else they need and following through may be needed. Paul was a man who recognised the need to follow through.

The first four verses are both like and unlike the beginning of the first letter. The address is the same. The first two verses are almost identical to the first letter: "the church of the Thessalonians in God and in Jesus Christ". As we have already seen, that is the opposite to how we would put it. We would say the church of God in Thessalonica. What is your address now? You are not the church of God in your town; you are the church of your town in God and in the Lord Jesus Christ.

Then come those two lovely greetings: "grace" is very like the Greek greeting; "peace" is the Hebrew greeting *shalom*. Shalom means health, harmony; the "peace of God", it has been said, *bypasses all misunderstanding*. The next part, vv. 3–4, have changed – because the Thessalonians have changed. If a Christian has not changed between letters, something is wrong. You can only go in two directions in the Christian life, forward or backwards, there is no in between. You cannot stand still and if you have been standing still then you have in fact been going back, because Christ has moved on and the world has moved on and unless you have moved on with Christ then you have in fact fallen back. You are no longer as close to him as you were.

Paul thanks God because they have gone forward since he had last written. It was probably only a few months before he wrote again, yet in those few months he had heard wonderful things. Their faith was growing more and more. The love in each of them for all of them was increasing by leaps and bounds. There is no joy greater to a minister of God than to see his converts going on, to see them getting bigger in spiritual stature, to see their faith getting stronger and their love getting deeper. It is a tremendous joy and you thank God for it because only God can do it, only he can give you life, and only he can help you to go on growing.

So Paul says, "We have just got to give thanks to God for you." Why is he so emphasising that? Frankly, because he has got to criticise them and it is always good psychology and good theology to thank God for something good in a person before you bring up the bad things. We can learn a lot from Paul here. Judicious praise can often do what indiscriminate criticism cannot do, and Paul knew that very well. Now he says, "Not only have you increased," but (v. 4), "We actually boast about you." There is a place for boasting in the Christian life, a place for being proud. You will find again and again in Paul's letters that he says, "I am proud of you; I boast of you when I am in another church – I say look at those Thessalonians."

When Paul was in Corinth or Athens or wherever, he would say: look at those Thessalonians – if you want to see what a church is really like then I will boast about those. He did not boast to the world. That would not have been fitting. But having thanked God that God was doing it, he was prepared to boast to the other churches.

When I was in other countries I would boast about my own church. I was not afraid, embarrassed or ashamed to do so. I would boast about them because it is God who does it. It is right to be proud if God is giving increase, because we may plant and someone else may water but it is only God who can help your faith to go on growing and your love to go on deepening.

So Paul really pats them on the back and gives them something to live up to, but if he was going to boast about them elsewhere, they had got to be right. So now, he is going to put them right. It is a lovely, tactful way to begin. He is saying: I boast about the way you face persecutions and make something positive of them. The most that the unbeliever can do with problems is defiantly to face them or, in a resigned way, to accept them. But the word Paul uses here means to take your sufferings and do something positive with them in such a way that the sufferings become your ally and not your enemy.

Here is a simple illustration: imagine somebody started throwing bricks at me and all I did was catch them and start building an extension with them. That is the word that Paul uses. Use your sufferings, use your troubles, catch them, and use them to help you to grow in faith. He is saying: that is what I boast about – your very problems, your very trials, you catch and you make them into something positive, and you build your faith up on them and you strengthen your nerve and your courage; I boast about you because you know how to handle difficulties.

Then he moves on to the main thing he wants to say in chapter one. "Your present suffering is proof of God's fairness." Now that is the most extraordinary statement when you think it through. The extraordinary thing is that most of us think it is just the opposite; if we have to suffer, we say, "Why do I have to suffer? What have I done to deserve this?" We never say that God is very fair to let me suffer like this; this is a very just thing. But do you realise that it is the fact that if you don't suffer, that is unfair? Why should you not suffer? You have sinned, haven't you? Yet we say, "God it is so unfair to do this." That is not how the New Testament talked. They knew that you must face suffering from God in this life or the next. Which do you want it in? Do you want your chastening here or do you want your punishment hereafter? Whom the Lord loves he chastises. "If you are not chastised by the Lord you're a bastard," says Hebrews 12, you are not his son at all.

You see for the believer, for the child of God, there is no suffering whatever after death, but there is real suffering before death. "It is through great tribulation that we must go to enter the kingdom of God."

"He who would live a godly life will suffer persecution." These very sufferings are God's badge of honour. They are his proof to you that you really are his child. A genuine father does punish his child. Do not believe that a father who never punishes his children is a loving father, he is not. But praise be to God, when he lets his children suffer here then that is a proof to them that he is being fair and that he is not going to let them suffer hereafter.

The thing to worry about is not if you suffer but if you don't, for it is the unbeliever who does not suffer from the world itself. It is the unbeliever who fits, it's the unbeliever who has a good time, and he may die peacefully in old age and they may look at him in his coffin and say, "Hasn't he a peaceful expression?" But for him suffering has just begun when he dies. Which would you rather have? Would you rather have the Lord's hand of chastening on you now to prove to you that you are a child of his, or would you rather have no suffering in this life and then face not chastening as a child of God but the retribution that belongs to sinners? That is the choice, but God is perfectly fair if he chastises me here. More than that, it is proof to me that I am on the way.

Therefore the New Testament does not say "Why should we suffer?" – the New Testament disciples thought it an honour. They rejoiced that they were worthy to suffer. Again that story comes back so clearly to my mind of people who were put in prison in Nepal because they were baptised. Seven of them were put in prison and the news came back to a prayer meeting in India. They began to pray, "Lord these poor Christians suffering in Nepal, release them. Set them free." As they prayed around the circle it came to an Indian woman and she prayed, "Lord, why did you give them the honour of suffering for you, and not us? Why should they have this privilege and not us? Why should they go to prison and you don't give us this blessing?" The whole tone of the prayer meeting changed, and the people realised that from their comfort and safety they had assumed that God's will for every Christian is comfort and safety.

But it is safety in the next world. He did not promise safety in this world. It is comfort in the next world; he did not promise an easy passage here. Jesus was utterly honest. As a missionary to the Muslim world (and that is the toughest mission field in the world) once said, "Christ never hid his scars to win a disciple." Do you understand that statement? Know it is tough. To become a Christian is not to get rid of your problems, it is simply to exchange one set of problems for another. Let no one be in any delusion about this, otherwise as soon as the first trouble comes a person's faith is shaken. But they had been told. Paul told his converts: don't you accept Christ unless you expect trouble. He told them that and I tell you that.

Paul is saying: count it as proof that you are on the right road that you are having trouble. He is so thrilled that he boasts about them. They have recognised that suffering is the badge of the Christian, and that if they are going to be buried with Christ and raised with Christ and identified with Christ, then the equivalent of the marks of the nails need to appear in the believers too. He suffered and we are called to do the same.

This is the deepest argument for a life after death. One of the arguments for a world to come is just this: that this world is so unfair. It is. Read Psalm 72 to get the real heartache of a man who said: I cleanse my heart in vain. I have agonies, I have pains, I go through problems and look at these wicked men. They are peaceful, they are well fed, and they die in their beds. It is a problem, isn't it? We feel it again and again – the unjust circumstances of this world. The good people are not always the ones who have health and wealth. Bad people often do, and it seems so unfair. There must be another world in which the wrongs are righted and in which the balance is restored. I know that Communists said of Christians, "You just made it up to compensate for the inequalities because you are not prepared to put right the inequalities in this world." That was how they talked. "You have to think of another world in which everything will be put right; it's delusion," they said, "pie in the sky when you die." My reply was always, "That's better than pain in the pit when you flit."

Paul is going to say that in fact there is another world and there is coming a great reversal of human fortune. There is coming a turning upside-down (or rather right way up) of the whole affair, the whole world situation in which those who

113

do not know God and who do not obey the gospel are going to suffer terribly and in which those who have suffered for Christ here are going to be at rest. When you walk around the cemetery now and see how often that word "rest" comes, you can understand the man who walked around the cemetery and then asked the grave digger where they buried all the sinners in that town. Because you never see on a gravestone that this man is suffering, that this man has gone to the wrong place. Well where do they bury all the sinners? Or do they cremate them all? What about the fact that most of the population of England gets a Christian burial and has said over them the words, "In sure and certain hope of the resurrection to eternal life..."? Are people living under the deception that everybody is all right as soon as they die? That is the hope of the world and it is a hope without any foundation. The hope of the world is that if there is any life after death then everybody is all right; that if there is a heaven, we will all scrape into it. If there is a hell it is only for Hitler!

Look now at the great reversal Paul portrays. It is the nearest anybody else in the New Testament (other than Jesus) came to talking about hell. People ask me, "Why do you believe in hell? Don't you think it's out of date?" or, "Don't you think it's a distortion of the simple gospel of Jesus coming to teach the love of God?" My reply is, "There is only one person I get my doctrine of hell from, and it is not anyone in the Old Testament, it is the person of Jesus. The one who had more love for people than anybody else. The one who cared more – he is the one who talked about hell and he made it quite clear." Somebody has said that everybody's dustbin (or garbage can) is an argument for hell. Why? What do you have a dustbin for? To put in that which is of no use to you. We put less in our dustbins with recycling, but there will still be things that we put in the bin because they are no use to us any more. It will then be taken away and burnt. In the ancient city of Jerusalem they did not have dustbins, they did not have refuse disposal facilities such as we have. But they did have a very deep valley on the south side of Jerusalem and all the rubbish was carried in buckets to the wall and tipped over the wall, and it tumbled down into that dark valley. Down there were men employed to keep that place burning and to keep that rubbish heap to manageable size. What the fires did not burn the maggots ate. Jesus said, "If you want to know what hell is like, look over the wall down that valley, that Valley of Hinnom, the Valley of Gehenna that is what it is like. Where the flame never dies out and the worm never stops eating." It is a sober and very sad picture.

You find little about hell anywhere other than on the lips of Jesus. It means that there could come a time when a human being made in the image of God to be useful to God reaches the point where God says, "This person is no more use to me." That moment will come as soon as a man or woman dies, though he may not be thrown into hell for a long time afterwards, not until judgment day. But it is in this life that we either prove useful to God or useless. It is in this life that we begin to be his children or we lose the opportunity ever to become his child. It is in this life that we decide where we will spend eternity. You cannot get around the teaching of the Bible on that. You may hope for a second chance after death. It is a vain hope. There is no scripture that allows you to hope that.

Instead there is a great gulf fixed the second you die that can never be crossed. These are solemn thoughts but Paul takes them up here. He uses words that should make our blood run cold, like "destruction", "exclusion", "vengeance" and the worst word of all is "everlasting". Let those words sink in. I know they are not nice. I know that you do not get all excited about them. I know that they rather give you a little shiver up your spine, but I would not be a preacher of the gospel if I did not say these things. I would be untrue to those to whom I preach. I could not face God and have him say to me, "Why did you skate over those verses? Why did you not tell them the whole truth? They need to know not only the joys of heaven but the horrors of hell."

Look at the word "everlasting". It means that when God's court has settled your destiny there can be no further appeal for there is no higher court. Do you understand that? If I go before a human court and I am found guilty and sentenced, I can appeal to a higher court. If I am found guilty in the Magistrate's Court, I can appeal to the Crown Court. If I am found guilty there, I can appeal ultimately to the Supreme Court. But when you come to God there is no higher so you are stuck. You can't appeal. To be cut off from God is hell, it really is.

I do not think people realise what it is to be cut off from God. People say, "Well look, I've lived in this world without God, I'll manage all right there. I'm fairly happy here. Why shouldn't I be happy there?" There are plenty of jokes about hell, making it seem a very happy place. But I will tell you why: because you do not realise that the goodness in this world is due to the fact that this world is not entirely separated from God, and God's grace is still working on human nature and therefore there is still goodness. But when you are separated from God, you are separated from goodness. The image that you were made in ceases to be capable of reflecting any of the goodness of the one whose image you bear. The result is that in hell there will be no love, no patience, no kindness, no goodness, no meekness, no self-control. I tell you there is not a zoo in the world that is so beastlike as hell will be. There won't be an animal in it, just people. It is a horrible picture and Paul uses the term "flaming fire" as our Lord did and we dare not get around that. Who will go there? Paul mentions two groups. Ask yourself now: "Am I in one of these groups?"

Group number one is those who do not know God; group number two is those who do not obey the gospel. Do you notice that no-one goes to hell because they do not know the gospel? That is important. In other words, if you have never heard the gospel, if you know nothing about Jesus Christ, you go to hell if you don't know God. Oh, but that's not fair. Surely what chance have they had to know God? The answer is that God has been trying to get to know them and has been speaking to them and has been getting through to them through the creation that he has made, through the conscience that he has put within them, he has been trying to get to know them. They could have known him. According to the Bible, if you are an atheist or an agnostic you have had to talk yourself into that position. You have had to suppress the evidence that you can see with your own eyes. Do you think that all this universe, and the planets and the stars, just happened by itself out of nothing? You have got to have a lot of faith to believe that. You have got to talk yourself – to brainwash yourself – to believe it. But when you look at all this, when you look at everything else, you say someone must have made it. Imagine I said to you about a book: "That book just happened; a bit of paper got together with a bit of ink and then met a cover" – it would be absolute folly. Yet there are people who will look at our universe which is a billion, billion, billion times as complex, and they say, "Well a little bit of interstellar dust met another little bit and there was a big bang and here we are." It is ludicrous. They know not God – not because they could not guess there was a God but because they did not want there to be one. So, some of those who have never heard the gospel go to hell because they would not get to know the God who wanted to get to know them. He spoke to them even in their hearts and in

117

their consciences about his standards.

It is intriguing that even in societies that have never heard the Ten Commandments people have believed some of those commandments. Where did they get it from? The Bible says that God wrote it in their hearts.

The other group that go to hell are those who have heard the gospel but do not obey it. You are not asked in the Day of Judgment, "Did you go to such and such a church and hear that preacher?" You are not asked, "Did you hear the gospel?" You are not asked, "Have you read your Bible?" You are asked, "Did you obey the gospel?"

What do you mean "obey the gospel"? I mean: what did you do about it?

"Well, what should I do about it other than go along and listen to sermons?" The answer is very simple. What is it to "obey the gospel"? – repent and be baptised every one of you for the forgiveness of your sins. Those who obey not the gospel are those who just do not do what the gospel says.

Let me turn away from this serious side. If the future world brings retribution for these two groups of people, the future world brings rest for those who have suffered for the Lord here. The book *Serge* is the story of a Russian boy who died some years ago but had been in the Russian secret police. His job had been to lead the bands of men who went into Christian meetings in homes, to beat up the Christians and to drag them to prison. Serge would take this trained bunch of thugs from the cage and go into homes and find twenty young people praising Christ, and he would beat them up.

He tells the story of how in one meeting they burst in and there was an attractive girl of about twenty-one and they beat her up on the table and left her bruised and bleeding and broken. Three weeks later he went into another part of that town and broke into a Christian meeting and there she was back again, singing. They beat her up again. Three weeks later or so he went to another Christian meeting and there she was again praising God. He could never forget that girl. That was one of the ways in which God got through to him. Finally, from a Russian ship in the Pacific Ocean, he swam miles to the Canadian shore to get away and start a life in Christ – it is a tremendous story.

I tell you that although those Russian persecutors (not Serge, he has been forgiven by the grace of Christ) will suffer terribly in the next world, those Christians who suffered for the name of Jesus will have rest, relief, and something more. It says that when Jesus comes back, the amazing thing that will happen is this: we shall not only see his face unveiled – we can't see it now it is veiled, there is a curtain hanging – one day it is as if the curtain will be pulled aside, and on the stage of history there will be Jesus in the centre where he is now. He is on the stage of history now in the centre, but he is veiled.

But at the unveiling the strange thing that will happen will be that when you see his face for the first time and realise exactly what he looks like, you will turn in amazement to your fellow Christians to say, "Doesn't he look marvellous, wonderful?" To your utter astonishment your fellow Christians will have the same face and look exactly like him. You will turn to other people and you will see they look exactly like him. The world will be utterly amazed. They will see a race like Christ in appearance and in fact, Paul says here that those who have suffered with him below, when they see him he will be admired in them, and the world will be amazed at what they see.

Part of Arthur Blessitt's story is remarkable. He and a friend were walking by a lake in America late one night and praying. Suddenly Arthur looked out over the lake and there was the figure of Jesus walking on the water towards him. He thought he was seeing visions. He could not believe it was real and so he did not say anything to his friend, but he kept looking again and the figure was walking nearer. Then he suddenly realised the friend could see him too and together they saw Jesus. That explains Arthur's ministry and the reality of Christ in his life and ministry. But then he went home that night and went through his own front door to the flat where he lived with his wife, and she took one look at his face, screamed, ran into the bedroom, slammed the door and locked it and would not let him in. He had to spend the night on the settee in the living room. In the morning he asked, "Why did you do that?" She replied, "Well, your face. It was all shining. It wasn't you." Later in the day he met his friend, and found that he had exactly the same experience. His wife, too, had not been able to look.

But one day, when we see Jesus as he is, we shall be like him, and people will look. They will be amazed. "There is Mrs Brown from down the road, look at her face, just like his! There's Mr Smith, look at his face, just like his!" What a future there is for those who suffer with him here. As he went through suffering to glory, we shall do the same. Therefore it is proof that we are chosen of God, that we are allowed the honour of suffering, of maybe even bearing in our body the marks of the Lord Jesus as Paul did, of making up the sufferings of Christ in one's own flesh. That does not mean making up anything that was lacking in his but making up what is lacking in ours, in conformity to his – it is a tremendous conception.

So Paul prays for the Thessalonians, and he says, "I pray that you may be worthy of all this." That God may look down at you and say: wasn't it worth it when we called him? Wasn't it worth it when we called her? That is what it means to be worthy, to be worth it all. Do you honestly feel that if God looked at your life now he would be able to say, "Oh wasn't it worth it?" For the Lord Jesus to look at you and think of his cross and his dying, and say, "Wasn't it worth it?" That you may be worthy and that every good intention you have may be brought to fruition in him. That is a tremendous prayer because Paul knew that the road to hell is paved with good intentions that were never kept. How many of us, in days of weariness or danger or sickness have said, "God, if you get me through this you've got all of me!" We made a good resolve and we had a good intention in our hearts. Perhaps you have been to a baptismal service and there has been a resolve made in your heart: "I must be baptised; I must go the whole way with Jesus." Or you have been alone with the Lord and the Lord has put his finger on something and said, "You know, you would be a better Christian if we got this right" and you made the resolve, "Yes, I'm going to do that." How many of those resolves got lost on the way? Paul is saying: I pray that you may be worthy and that every good intention, every resolve, is brought to pass, that Jesus' name may be glorified in you and you in him all by his grace.

You see there is one secret through it all, and that is grace. You never do it by grind. We often think we will get there by working so hard and by trying to be a better Christian. It is not trying, it is trusting; it is not wrestling, it is nestling. It is *trusting* to be good and letting him complete the work. It is the grace of God and our Lord Jesus Christ. The great divide comes, and notice there are only two destinies. The Bible mentions no third position. There is no middle way. There are those who face the flaming fire of eternal destruction, which does not mean annihilation, it means utter ruin; and there are those who face rest, and who will be transformed into the same glory so that they bear the image of the Lord again. Those are the only two destinies.

The sad truth is that God alone knows exactly which destiny faces every person. I think of a baptismal service. The candidates have begun the Christian life. They want to have their faith increase, they want to have their love deepen, and they want to go on so they are taking the step of baptism. It is a step that is one step on the road that leads to glory and leads to the lovely future that I have mentioned. It is a step that is burying the old person with the old face, in order that one day they might be the likeness of Christ. It is a right step, a holy step. But to the candidates we say that we do not baptise them into their own names. We baptise them into Jesus Christ. It is his name they bear and we do it in order that his name may not be discredited but glorified in them and that they may be glorified in him.

8

Read 2 Thessalonians 2:1–12

A. ARRIVAL OF LORD STILL FUTURE (1–5)

1. PRECIOUS RETURN OF CHRIST
   a. Appearing Saviour
   b. Assembling saints

2. Previous rebellion of antichrist
   a. Destroying religion
   b. Demanding reverence

B. ACTIVITY OF DEVIL ALREADY PRESENT (6–12)

1. Mystery of lawlessness restrained
   a. Regulative principle (it)
   b. Representative person (he)

2. Man of lawlessness revealed
   a. Deceiving signs
   b. Deluded sinners

There have been bad times through the centuries of the history of our earth, but I think this must be the first generation to be living with the possibility of the end of the world within the foreseeable future. I walked into a College of Technology and a young man was operating a computer, programming it for something. I asked, "What are you working on?" He replied, "I'm trying to work out the date of the end of the world" – and he was serious. He was trying to repeat the experiment that had been done in Massachusetts Institute of Technology, in which six hundred different equations of food, population and hundreds of other factors were fed into the machine, and it was asked, "How much longer have we before crossover point?"

Many years ago now I read the notes of a lecture given by a UN expert, entitled *Prospects for Survival*. We live with this problem. There are two reactions that people are having. Some are panicking, becoming very fearful; others are running away and burying their head in the sand, saying, "I don't want to look. I can't bear to think of the future; I'm just going to live for now and hope that I can survive and die before it all drops on us." We are having to live with the possibility of the end of the world.

I have known a great switch in the thinking of young people as I go into schools and colleges. Years ago they never asked me about the end of the world; now it is a constant question and our young people are having to live with the knowledge. Of the people who are thinking about it and wanting to get ready for the future, some are turning to science for the answer and some are turning to superstition. Some turn to science and study what is called "futurology", while others read the stars, and study horoscopes.

Science does not have the answer to the future, and superstition does not have the answer either, but scripture does. The Bible brings you down to earth and up to heaven, both with a lovely surprise. It seems to bring reality into your thought about the future. Whatever is happening to your feelings, the scripture sticks to facts, and it is a great help to have the facts laid before you.

Now 2 Thessalonians 2 gives you a number of facts and I want to put them in their setting. These facts were written down because people had got them wrong, and there is no happier hunting ground for the crank than the teaching of Christians about the future. Many of the sects and cults which knock on your door have all kinds of weird and wonderful notions about the future. Of course, since the future has not happened, we are free to speculate. Thank God we do not need to, if we know our Bibles. Let us stick to the facts as they are clearly laid out in the Word; let us not go beyond the Word in what it says. If it is there, God wants us to know it; if it's not there, he does not.

In Thessalonica, Paul, from the very beginning of preaching Christianity to them, had told them that Christ was going to come back again to this planet. It is a vital part of Christian thinking, the centre of our hope. It provides the anchor for us to hold onto when the storm hits us. We have an anchor within the veil – our hope – and we hold onto that anchor. But Paul is saying to the Thessalonians: you are getting shaken from your moorings; the anchor is loosening, and you are becoming panic stricken; you are getting unbalanced, overexcited. People can get overexcited and unbalanced in matters of the second coming of our Lord Jesus Christ.

One of the saddest cases I heard of was a girl who used to spend her spare time in cemeteries so that she would be with the dead when they rose to meet the Lord in the air. I am sure the Lord did not want her to do that; the living would catch up with the dead quickly enough, but she had got it wrong, out of balance. It is very easy to get matters of the second coming out of proportion. This is what had happened at Thessalonica: they had got the fundamental facts right: the appearing of the Saviour and the assembly of the saints. These are the two fundamental facts: Jesus is coming back, and when he does, we will meet him.

You wait till you get there – it will be a huge crowd. We will all be there who know and love the Lord. Now these are facts: the Lord is coming back; we are going to meet him in the air and before his feet even touch the earth we will be with him. Those who have been dead in Christ for centuries will be there. All the Christians who are alive will leave their place where they are, and they will go to be with him. Don't ask me how it will all happen – you will not believe it is happening. If you have not had a chance to go and visit the Holy Land, it is coming for you and you will look right down on the Holy City from above the Mount of Olives. I love looking at aerial photographs of Jerusalem because I think, "That is how it will look; that is what we will see." How marvellous!

The Thessalonians had got the basic facts right but something else wrong. Satan hates the doctrine of the second coming. Why? Because when Jesus comes, Satan has to go. He will have to leave his sphere of power. He is the god of this world, the prince of this world, the ruler of this world – and the moment Jesus comes back, Satan has to get out and he knows it. If he can twist Christians' ideas of the second coming, he will. If he can switch you away from the simple Bible facts about this great event, he will. We are not ignorant of his devices.

Satan hates this subject. It is why if he can get Christians off it, he will. If he cannot get them off it, he will push them too far into it and get them all tied up with charts and get it out of balance. They had got it out of balance in

Thessalonica. What had they got out of balance? How had Satan managed to get them all panicked about it? Well, there are three ways that Satan can get through to Christians and alter their understanding. One is false prophets, and Paul mentions that first. Second, there is misinterpreted scripture, and that is a thing that every preacher is mortally afraid of doing. It would be better for me to have a millstone around my neck and jump into the river than to mislead one of the Lord's little ones by misinterpreting scripture. "Be not many teachers," says James, knowing that they will go through the greater judgment. Yes, if you have taught others it is a horrible responsibility. The third way in which Christians can be misled is by forgeries. Paul knows they may have had a forged letter purporting to come from him, signed "Paul". Satan is up to all kinds of tricks and he will stoop to anything. He will stop at nothing to mislead Christians and twist their ideas about the second coming. So he will give false prophecies, get teachers to misinterpret the Bible, and he will even forge documents that will mislead. Paul tells them not to listen to any of this.

If that was how Satan had misled the Thessalonians, what in particular had they been taught that was wrong? The answer is they had been taught that Jesus could come again any moment, without warning. That is not biblical teaching, and 2 Thessalonians 2 could not be clearer – certain things have to happen first. So a Christian should not panic. You should not be in mortal fear that he might come tonight and take your family without you. That is the kind of panic to which the apostles made no appeal whatever. So this theory had been given to the Thessalonians and, worse than that, they had been told not only can he come at any moment without warning, but he is already on his way and the day of the Lord has already started – that we are in it. In 1 Thessalonians, the first epistle, they were afraid that the dead were going to miss Christ's coming. Now they were afraid that those who were alive had missed it.

The Thessalonians were now worried not only that those who died were not going to be there when Christ came, but were frightened that he was already somehow coming and they were missing it. Paul encourages them to calm down and get back to the facts. He could hardly be plainer, hardly simpler. I just want to tell you that every teaching on the second coming you hear must line up perfectly with 2 Thessalonians 2 if you are to believe it. There it says that before the Lord comes, certain events have to take place. It is only when those events take place that you need begin to get ready. Of course, you should be ready any time, for your personal call in death may come at any moment. That is the one you should be ready for. But we should be watching and praying so that when we see the fig tree begin to bud and blossom, we look up, for the day of our redemption draws nigh. That is what we are watching for – certain events. When these events begin to appear, as they are doing, then we know we are getting much nearer.

Paul never believed that Christ would come at any moment in his life, but he did hope that he would come before he died. It was the heart of his desire that he should never have a funeral but step straight from this world into the next and meet Jesus in the air. Paul was disappointed in that hope, as many generations since have been. I have that hope; every Christian has that hope. I hope it will be within my lifetime.

It would be super to have that, but it will not come suddenly; it won't come as a thief in the night to Christians. We are awake. We are not of the night; we are not drunk as those who drink at night. "We're sober," says Paul in 1 Thessalonians 5. It will not surprise you; it will not overtake you like a thief in the night. You will be ready. You will see the events; you will know that it is coming.

What are the events that have to happen before Jesus comes back? First, the precious return of Christ must be preceded by the previous rebellion of Antichrist. Here we are introduced to a fundamental teaching of the Bible about the future. One day there is going to be one man, the most powerful man in the world, a tool of Satan, dominating the world scene. He will be a dreadful man and yet he will be welcomed by the world. Before Christ can come, Antichrist must come. Until he has come, we cannot expect Christ back. It could not be plainer. Paul says that the Antichrist must appear. There will be a rebellion, a period of apostasy, falling away from God. Into that vacuum will step one human being, totally in the hands of Satan, an incarnation of evil. That one human being will be the most dominating figure of history. It is intriguing that the devil once offered Jesus the post of Antichrist. He said, "If you would bow down and worship me, I'll give you all the kingdoms of the world." Jesus didn't say, "They are not yours to give." They were, and Satan will one day give them to his Antichrist and that man will rule the whole world.

We know that he will do two things towards religion. First, he will destroy religion. Secondly, he will demand reverence of himself as god. This has been the pattern in every totalitarian regime. Those who have wanted to be dictators and totally control people have found this: that they can control bodies by sheer military force; they can control their minds with propaganda, but they cannot control the spirits of those who believe in the living God. They have tried. Therefore, since they are frustrated and therefore, only controlled two-thirds of people, they try to step into the religious sphere. They do it first by trying to ban religion. As atheistic, communistic Russia tried to ban religion and failed miserably; they tried to get hold of this other part of man and they could not do it. Then, having destroyed religion and created a God-shaped blank in the human soul, as Huxley described it, they must then fill it with something else because people are incurably religious.

It is intriguing that under the old communist regimes in eastern Europe they had to introduce secular ceremonies of christening, marriage, and burial to replace the spiritual ceremonies which they banned. They had to replace God with the state. They had to replace the religious blank with a god that is human. Almost every dictator has done this and it went to his head and he thought he was God. Nebuchadnezzar in Babylon said, "Is not this great Babylon which I have built by my power in my kingdom for my glory? Mine is the kingdom, the power, and the glory." God said, "No it's not," and Nebuchadnezzar went mad that very day and only recovered his sanity when he came back to God.

Dictator after dictator has said, "I'm God; bow down; worship me." Millions have bowed down and worshipped men. Fame goes to pop stars' heads; they can have youngsters who are giving them the place, the attention and affection that ought to be given to God alone. But what happens when such temptations get too much? Do you remember the year that one of the Beatles said, "We are now as famous as Jesus Christ"? Did you shudder for the Beatles when they said that? Where are they now? So, "God sits in heaven and laughs," says Psalm 2. The nations rage, but God laughs for he will have the last word.

But this man of lawlessness, this Antichrist, this human figure, will destroy religion and replace it by himself, putting an image of himself in the very temple of God in Jerusalem, and saying, "I am God; worship me." Something like this was done by that horrible figure Antiochus Epiphanes. It was done by the emperor Caligula. One of the claims of the Roman Caesars was to be God, so they called themselves "lord" and they said, "Bow down and say, 'Caesar is lord,' to us." The only people who would not do so were the Jews and the Christians. The Jews were legally excused from doing so, but the Christians were not. The Christians who said, "We will not say, 'Caesar is lord,' for Jesus is Lord," paid the supreme penalty and died for it. Just three words signed their death warrant.

There have been many attempts to identify Antichrist throughout history. The popes have been named, Napoleon was called Antichrist, as Stalin and Hitler were. I think none of these was the Antichrist. Later we will see what they were and explain why people have appeared in history who looked like Antichrist but proved not to be. But I want to underline the false teaching of Christ coming at any moment and our disappearing from the world scene before Antichrist calls himself God. I believe that to be very misleading. The idea was first mooted in the nineteenth century among a group of sincere but rather unbalanced Christians, called the "Irvingites", and came as a prophecy which was not tested by the scripture. Henry Irving, the leader, went to Dublin where he was heard by a man called J. N. Darby who then taught it to an American, Dr C. I. Scofield, who put it in the Scofield Annotated Bible. From there it has spread far and wide.

We have a flood of books coming from the USA with this teaching of a secret disappearance of all Christians before the Antichrist comes. I just want to say: "2 Thessalonians 2!" Paul, calming the panic, is removing the wrong emotions from the situation. Look at facts: Christ cannot come until Antichrist has come and called himself God. So do not let anyone mislead you, any preacher, any teacher. Always check what I have said by the Word of God. I beg you in the name of the Lord. Never say, "David Pawson said...." Look into your Bible and see if God said it. If God said it, believe it. If I am wrong, for the good of my soul tell me I am wrong.

But I beg you, take 2 Thessalonians 2 very seriously, "He must first be revealed, then...."

If the Antichrist has not yet appeared, and therefore Christ cannot yet appear or come, then are these not just future events which may have no relationship to us at all? How do we relate the future and the present together? The answer is in the second thing that Paul says in this twelve-verse passage. He says, "The activity of the devil is already present," or as we would say in modern language, "The trends that are leading to that climax can already be seen in our daily newspapers."

John says it in an epistle: "Many antichrists have gone out into the world, none of whom is the Antichrist." In other words, there have been human beings throughout history who have pointed forward to the Antichrist, giving us a glimpse of what he will be like, giving us a clue to the kind of thing he will do. I have mentioned Antiochus Epiphanes, Caligula, Nero and Domitian. Right through the middle ages, some of the popes did deserve the title of "antichrist" with a small "a". Then coming through to Napoleon, and Mussolini, and Stalin, they have all shown a bit of this.

Antichrist will offer peace without God. There are many people in lesser spheres (maybe you have one in the office) who can behave like Antichrist within their little reality. Wherever man thinks he is a god, it is the fundamental sin from the Garden of Eden. What did Satan say to Adam and Eve? "You will be like gods" – and that is what we want. The man at Cambridge who tutored Prince Charles, prepared him for his future life and gave him his basic philosophy, gave lectures on the BBC. He said, "Man has now come of age; he doesn't need God. He's divine."

We have been brought up in an age in which people think they are gods. We can put a man on the moon. God put man on the earth, we can start putting them somewhere else;

we think we have come of age, so we say. There are many antichrists and all this is heading up to just one human being who will gather all these threads into himself and say, "I am God; I recognise no laws above me." That is what is meant by the phrase "Man of Lawlessness". It doesn't mean a man who goes around committing crimes everywhere; it means a man who recognises no law except his own will.

What was the great crisis over President Nixon? Why do I personally believe that President Ford made a very big mistake in pardoning President Nixon? There was a quite profound and wonderful article in *Time* magazine called *The Theology of Forgiveness*. Whoever wrote it really understood the Bible for he said: "You cannot forgive until there is confession and repentance. To forgive before there is, is to destroy the recognition that everybody is under law." Now, that is a profound statement. Is the President of the United States under law or on top of it? That was the deep principle being debated. Antichrist will say, "There is no law, but the laws I make." You thank God if you live in a country where leaders acknowledge laws above themselves. The UN Declaration of Human Rights is at least an attempt of the nations to say that there are principles above us, under which we live. When the rulers of a nation do not recognise moral laws above themselves, you have the Antichrist spirit – the spirit of lawlessness – coming. For the real spirit of lawlessness is not necessarily to break laws, it is just to fail to recognise laws. It is a spirit that is sweeping through our land at this moment. "Who is going to tell me what to do? My parents are not going to make laws for me. My school is not going to tell me what to do. The university authorities aren't going to tell us students what to do. We are going to make our own laws."

Antichrist will be the epitome of this attitude, recognising none of God's commandments, none of the moral principles which God has said he has built this universe upon, and will say instead, "I make the laws; I am the law." It is a terrible prospect, but that is what is coming.

But Paul says that this mystery of lawlessness is at the moment restrained. Thank God it is and that somebody is keeping the brakes on. Now who or what? Here is one of the more difficult questions in this chapter. In one sentence, Paul calls this restraining factor an "it" and in the next sentence, "he". On the one hand, he writes of something impersonal; on the other hand, he talks of something personal. There have been many debates about what he means or who he means: restraining evil, holding back the spirit of lawlessness. What is it? Who is it? I believe the answer is it is both a "what" and a "who" and that they are closely related.

What—I believe that the regulative principle of law and order is the "what". Thank God if you live in a land of law and order. It is God's brake on society. It is God's brake on men who want to be a law to themselves; it is God's way of stopping them. It is God who gives human beings a sense that there are certain universal principles to be observed in society and in our relationships with one another. It is God who has put that principle into our society, and Romans 13 makes that clear. So that the first thing we can say about the restraining factor on lawlessness is: law, and God has given it.

When King Alfred wrote the first book of English law, at the head of it he wrote the Ten Commandments. Now that is a mixed thing to do. I am not sure that it is absolutely right and no policeman has ever been able to apply the tenth commandment to any person. Nevertheless, he was recognising that God's commandments are above us. When the Queen of England was crowned in Westminster Abbey, she was given the Bible and this was said: "Here is the royal law" – meaning here is the law for you; you are under law.

This is the royal law, the law of the King of kings for earthly kings and queens.

But it is not just a principle, for law must always be represented in a person. When a policeman stops you, the law has stopped you. You are in the hands of the law. Just one constable and you are in the hands of the law. When you go to court there is a judge. When he wears the wig, he is renouncing his personality. In fact, they were originally worn so that the criminals would not recognise the judge outside the court and get their own back. He wears it in a sense to become rather impersonal. But he is a person who embodies the law. When he condemns you, it is the law that has condemned you. In other words, God's pattern is that the principle of law to restrain lawlessness is embodied in a "he". It is so in a household and every father is ultimately responsible for the discipline of his own household.

Who then is Paul thinking of when he refers to he who embodies this restraining principle? He could be referring to the Roman emperor of his day who embodied the law. He could be referring to any head of state who embodies the law for that state or society. Or he could be referring to something even deeper. Behind the judge is the law and behind the law is the Holy Spirit of God. I believe that one of the functions of God the Holy Spirit clearly described in scripture is the restraining of lawlessness in human society and that if God ever decides to withdraw his Spirit from human society then lawlessness will follow immediately, and it has happened once. You can read all about it in Genesis 6. God looked down on the earth and what did he see? He saw all kinds of horrible things. He saw people living purely at a physical level: eating, drinking, and marrying, and just not living for God at all. He saw the results of that in their own character, personality, behaviour and conversation. He looked down and he said, "My Spirit is not going to strive with you forever." God was saying, "I am going to take the brakes off your society." What happened? Violence and anarchy filled the earth. God only has to withdraw his Holy Spirit from society generally. The brakes are off, the law is useless, and lawlessness prevails.

Do you realise that law-abiding citizens owe that to the Holy Spirit striving with them? He strives with them through their conscience, strives with them through their upbringing, strives with them through the discipline they have learned in school and college. The Holy Spirit is striving with society. But let that Holy Spirit withdraw, and when he who restrains lawlessness stops doing so, then the total situation becomes lawless. "As in the days of Noah, so in the days of the coming of the Son of Man" – when the Holy Spirit withdraws his striving with man, it is in that situation of anarchy and violence that the world will say, "Someone please give us peace and security."

When you have anarchy and violence the dictator steps in. We have seen it happen again and again. It could happen in our society for democracy is breaking down in the Western world and creating a political vacuum into which either right wing or left wing totalitarianism can so easily step. The strong man just waits to step in and say, "I'll give you peace and security, but you must accept me as dictator. You must accept my power and my will as law." Can't you see that happening in our world? Violence and anarchy are spreading throughout our world.

When I board a plane for another country, I know that I shall have to go through all those security things at the airport. I will be searched, felt all over, my luggage will be opened, I will have to go through electronic devices. Why? Because violence and anarchy are in the world, that is why. It is not even safe to travel now. That is the result of the Spirit being withdrawn. There is a parallel with the days of Noah.

The violence and the anarchy came before Noah got into the ark; they did not escape from that world until the violence had come. What Paul is saying in 2 Thessalonians 2 is that the Spirit will be withdrawn before you meet the Lord in the air and the man of rebellion will be revealed.

Now concerning this man of lawlessness. Every one of the three words that I use to describe the coming of Christ, I use to describe the coming of Antichrist. Transliterating the Greek into English words, they are: *parousia*, *epiphany* and *apocalypse*. Or, as I translate them for you: *a royal visit* – that is parousia; an *appearing* – that is epiphany or epiphaneia, if you want the Greek; and apocalypse – *unveiling*, drawing the curtain back on the stage. Those three very words are used here of Antichrist. He comes to imitate Christ. The word "anti" does not mean "against," it means "instead of".

This *instead of Christ*, this counterfeit Christ, this substitute Christ, we are told in the book of Revelation, will have the face of the Lamb. He will be a gentle, friendly person. We are told that he will perform miracles, signs, and wonders – counterfeit miracles to prove to people that he is supernatural. One of the things that will fool millions will be that he will do supernatural miracles. He will be a wonder boy, bringing peace and security. He will be a substitute Christ and he will deceive many people.

Do you remember when Moses went to Pharaoh God said, "What's that in your hand, a stick? When you get to Pharaoh, throw it down; it will become a snake." So Moses did this and Pharaoh looked. Do you know what happened? The occult black magicians of Egypt threw their sticks on the ground and they turned into snakes also. Satan can counterfeit miracles. He can counterfeit physical healing. He can counterfeit tongues. He can counterfeit prophecy. Any gift of the Spirit he can duplicate, and he will in Antichrist; it will fool a lot of people.

But let me tell you the end of the story of the snakes: Moses' snake swallowed up theirs. Christ will slay Antichrist with the breath of his mouth, and will blow him away just that easily. It only needs Christ to blow and Antichrist has left the scene. Many people in our world will accept the lie. Satan will have led them, they will have led themselves, and God will have led them. Paul is saying that, if you believe the lie of Antichrist: you will be to blame, Satan will be responsible, and God will have done it too.

That is an extraordinary statement, so let me explain. It begins with self. Think about this sentence: "Satan has no advantage over any of you except those which you have given him." Did you realise that? So it starts with self. Now how does anybody get into the position where Satan can give them the lie so plausibly, so impressively, that they believe it and they believe that Antichrist is the saviour of the world? I will tell you how. There are four steps and they are utterly clear.

Paul says it is because they have refused the truth. Why did they refuse the truth? Because they did not like it. Why did they not like it? Because they did not want to be saved. Why didn't they want to be saved? Because they delighted in wickedness. Now do you see that? That is logical and clear. Someone hears the truth of God and rejects it. Why? Because of intellectual difficulties? The Bible does not take that one – it is an excuse.

Why does someone who has had the truth explained to him, go away and forget it? Why does he argue with it? Why will I be in a local school one morning and have most of the top class in that school coming back at me, arguing with what I am saying, trying to disprove it, trying to say it is not true? Why do they get so angry about it? Why do they get so hot about it? I will tell you why: we reject the truth because we do not like it. Paul says that you do not love the truth. Why do we not love the truth? Because if we loved it we would be saved. But surely everybody wants to be saved? No, they don't. They take pleasure in unrighteousness. It all boils down to the simple fact that we enjoy being bad. Someone who enjoys being bad therefore does not want to be saved, therefore does not love the truth and therefore rejects it. The difficulty, you see, is not mental; no-one was ever kept away from God through lack of intelligence or through mental problems. Deep down, it is a moral problem.

The person who does that with his self is then wide open to Satan to give him the grand delusion. You know, Satan convinces a man with a brilliant intellect that Christianity is wrong. The man can argue himself into it and it is all logical to him. He cannot see the truth and Satan blinds his eyes. Then, after he has rejected the truth himself and Satan has blinded his eyes, it says God will then come along and push him further into the delusion. Why? Well, God is a just God. God says: if you choose that, I will help you along that way; if you have chosen that, I will help you with it as a punishment. What a terrible punishment, having chosen delusion, to have God push you further into it. But it is God's way of showing that there are only two sorts of people in the world: the sort who will accept Christ when he comes because they have loved the truth, and the sort who will accept Antichrist when he comes because they have not loved the truth.

What about those who have never heard of Christ? The Bible is quite clear about that. There is no problem about it. The Bible simply says they have received some truth through creation and conscience. If they have loved the truth they have already received, they will welcome Christ. Missionaries have known that happen. There are people who have never heard about Christ, but who have loved the truth, and when they have heard about Christ they have said, "Well that is the name I've been waiting to hear. I have loved him for years. Now you have told me who it was."

If you love the truth, you will welcome Christ when he comes. But if you do not love the truth, if you do not want to be saved, and if you are enjoying being a sinner, then frankly, when Antichrist comes you will welcome him. Everybody in a congregation will line up behind those two. There are two people coming to this world, two men: one from Satan, one from God – the Antichrist and the Christ. They will both appear; they are both coming. They are both going to have an epiphany; they are both going to have an apocalypse. Antichrist will come first, Christ second, and every one of us will welcome one or the other.

Do you love the truth? Do you want to be saved? Do you want to give up enjoying the things that God has forbidden? Then, Paul says, get ready. These things are already happening. The trends are already there. The mystery of lawlessness is already at work, permeating our society. He says that it is a secret because many people are not aware; they do not discern it. Christians do. They read their newspapers and say, "I can see it coming." The trends are there. There are many antichrists in the world already, preparing the way for one Antichrist. But praise God, you look over the whole world and there are millions of people who are preparing for Christ's coming. They have loved the truth and they are being saved and now they love righteousness. That is not to say they are perfect. No, they may still sin, but now they hate it when they do, because they love the truth.

9

Read 2 Thessalonians 2:13–3:5

A. DIVINE SOVEREIGNTY
1. He elects
    a. Work of Spirit   b. Word in scripture
2. He connects
    a. Gospel by Christians b. Glory of Christ
3. He perfects
    a. Encouragement by grace
    b. Established in goodness
4. He protects
    a. Girded in strength   b. Guarded from Satan
5. He directs
    a. Love to God   b. Loyalty to Christ

B. HUMAN RESPONSIBILITY
1. We stay
    a. Tradition of apostles b. Teaching in epistles
2. We pray
    a. Speed for message   b. Safety of messenger
3. We obey
    a. Confidence in Lord   b. Consistency in life

The end of chapter two is a very stark contrast to the beginning of it. In the beginning there is an air of pessimism and gloom. We have been thinking about Antichrist and the powers of evil that are already working in the world, what things are coming to, and the terrible things that still have yet to appear on earth, and we ought to be getting ready for these things. But suddenly at the end of chapter 2 Paul becomes optimistic. Why? Because, just as evil is already working in the world, and working towards a climax, so good is already working in the world and working towards a climax. Just as Antichrist is already being foreshadowed in the events of today, so the coming of Christ is being foreshadowed, and this is the Christian view.

I was once asked in a young people's meeting: "Are you a pessimist or an optimist about the future?" My answer is clear: "Both, because I'm a realist." I believe that the Christian view of the world is that the wheat and tares are growing together to a harvest. That is part of the problem – we have got to live with this mixed field, seeing the two intertwining. We have to live in a world that is a strange mixture of good things and evil things. They grow together, but they are both developing towards a climax. They grow maybe slowly and gradually so that we hardly notice them, but they are growing and ripening. One day they will be cut; they will both be cut out of this world, and the good will go to one place and the evil to another. It is mixed together now, but it will not stay that way.

So we are going to look now at the good that is happening in the world. It is the case that Satan is very busy in the world, capturing key men, gripping this world, so there is the spread of the tares in the field, which is God's world – but now we look at the bright side: God is working wonderfully. The good things are ripening too, and you can see what is happening. Our subject is predestination and free will. How about that? You can't go far in the Bible without coming up against the problem and the question. In fact, it is written into many pages of the Bible, but this passage is singularly appropriate to this question. At the end of this section you may be terribly dissatisfied with me and say that I have not answered the problem. Frankly, I will not have done. If I preach for another thousand years I would not answer the problem and you would still be left with the questions. I want to take you to a higher realm than this question. I want you to see these two things not as separate pillars standing on earth but as two separate pillars supporting a single archway above the clouds. There, in God's presence, you see the resolving of this tension in our thinking.

Let us start with divine sovereignty. You see, if anyone has got free will, God must have. The way we talk about human free will we are trying to say that God must have none, that it must all be our decision – we must have free will and we must choose everything. But God is a free God—if anyone has free will, God has. It is up to him to do what he likes and no man will ever stop him. So we start with divine sovereignty. It is the sovereignty of three persons so united in heart, mind and will that you can say, "They are one." Father, Son and Spirit are all mentioned in these few verses. The Father sent the Son, he sent the Spirit, and the Father has absolute free will.

One of the intriguing things about what God does here is this: it says that our Lord Jesus and God may do this, and then a number of things are listed. But every verb listed after that is in the singular. Do you get the message? When God and Jesus do something they act as one, and all the verbs are singular even though two subjects of the verb are acting – they are so close together.

There are five things that God does and they are all very simple. I have put them in an alliterative form so that you can simply check them off on your fingers.

First: God *elects* people. Paul says, "I want to thank God that he elected you, that he *chose* you...." Now, let us get this absolutely straight: no one *chooses* to be a Christian themselves. You cannot choose to do so – the initiative belongs to God alone. He sets the process in motion. It is he who comes to us. We are not in a position of having persuaded him to receive us; we are in the position where he has persuaded us to receive him. Now we must get that clear otherwise the foundation of your faith is in yourself and that is a weak foundation; your Christianity will collapse if you build on your will. Build it on God's will and you have got a solid foundation. It is God who chooses who will be a Christian. It is he who elects. It is an election, only it is God who puts the cross against a name.

I am only a teacher because God took the initiative and stepped into my life. I know on that Friday night, which I shall never forget, I thought I had accepted him, or rather, I thought I had chosen to be a Christian. But it was not long before I realised he had been getting through to me. I was not doing him a favour in coming to him and saying, "Right, you can count on me now, Lord. You have got another one." No, God had reached down in his mercy out of heaven, and he had started speaking to me. He had been trying to reach me before I was born because my parents prayed for me when I was still in the womb. As I look back now I can see he had been trying to reach me through faithful Sunday school teachers. They had a tough time Sunday after Sunday, but God was trying to reach me then. I can see that in contact after contact, God was choosing me and God was getting through. He was taking the initiative. God chooses.

So Paul says, "I thank God that he elected you Thessalonians." Do you notice that you can know who is elected? It is not a secret hidden thing that nobody can ever find out. You know! When it is one's privilege to see someone coming to the Lord, it is great to say, "God, you've chosen this person. You've got into their life. You've spoken to them. You want them to be your child – that is thrilling." You see, it has not been your work or your will persuading another will to accept Jesus. It has been the work of God. How have they done it? How did they reach that person? Paul says that it is through the work of the Spirit and the Word of the truth, which means the scripture. Wherever God is choosing people you will find he is choosing them through those two means.

In heaven, God and Jesus are choosing someone on earth. Then how do they get hold of them on earth? Through the working of the Spirit and through the Word of the scripture, that is how it is done. Either without the other makes an inadequate call. You see, there are those who have got the Word of scripture and they can quote texts, and they have got it all off, but where is the life? Where is the warmth? There are those who have had touches of the Holy Spirit and those who have felt the excitement of God's Spirit, and sung and waved their arms, but where is the Word of scripture?

If it is a call from God, and a call that is going to lay a solid foundation, you will find the Spirit and the scripture acting together in harmony – the one providing the heat and the other the light – that is how God chooses. Praise God wherever you see the Spirit moving, wherever you hear the scripture being expounded, it is there that you will find God choosing people because he sent those two factors. These are the two things on earth that correspond to the choice of the Father and Son in heaven. Is that a bit deep? Well, I believe it to be very simple really. Paul looks at that group of Christians in Thessalonica and says, "He elected you." That is where it began.

Secondly, God *connects* with us. He wants us to be in direct communication with him, and it is he who establishes the link. Paul mentions here the beginning of that connection and the end of it. The beginning of it is when you hear the gospel preached. You notice Paul says "our gospel" – it is a gospel that God has entrusted to human beings. The election has taken place years before you know it; centuries before the foundation of the world your name was written, but the connection takes place as soon as you hear the gospel. It will be someone's gospel because God in his mercy has not sent the gospel down from heaven, he has given the gospel on earth to people to pass on, and you could be the vital link in the chain to pass it on.

What is the end of that connection? It is that God should link you with the glory of Jesus in heaven. Now that glory, to be quite practical, is a light that is brighter than the midday sun. Paul saw the glory of Jesus on the Damascus road, and he saw it because he was the only apostle to meet Jesus after his ascension after he had gone back to glory. He saw a light brighter than the midday sun. So the beginning of the connection is the gospel and the end is the glory. In Daniel 12: "The righteous shall shine like stars." Have you ever wanted to be a star? You will be in Jesus! He connects you through the gospel and to the glory, and one day that will be shared by you.

The third thing God does is: he *perfects* us. When God starts a job he never leaves it half-done. Now what does he put into us, and why does he put it into us? Well, let us look at two things. We face a holy God whose standards are stricter than any of ours. God has *absolute* standards of morality, of holiness, of purity. If one thing is clear it is that human nature cannot reach absolute standards, and therefore we live by relative standards. We talk about "white lies" and that is a relative term. A lie in God's sight is always black. We talk about shades of grey; we talk about being "just over the line on the right side", but for God there are absolute standards.

Now here is the problem: how can a God of strict absolute standards live with me? Living with people who are different from yourself is always difficult, especially if their standards are lower than yours. Have you ever lived with someone whose standard of cleanliness was lower than yours or whose standard of cooking was poorer than yours? Can you imagine what it is like for God to have to live with sinners? The answer is that he cannot do it for very long. He can only do it for a time and that is why he set a limit to human life.

But God want us to live with him forever so he elects us, he then connects us through the gospel with the glory of Christ, and he then perfects us. When we try to encourage someone, we do so by lowering the standard to their level, do we not? We give them a kind of pass mark: "Judged on their standard". But God, being a holy God, cannot do this. He has to keep the standard at 100%. He cannot lower the standard, so what does he do? Sometimes holy people discourage you by simply expecting an impossible standard of you, don't they? But Jesus came not to lower the standard but to lift the people. He came to encourage us in goodness. It is by his grace. He did not just say, "You've got to get up here to live with me," he reached down a helping hand of grace to lift us up here.

So we have received "encouragement and good hope through grace," says Paul, "because he will establish us in all good deeds." He will do it. It is his work to perfect us, and that is a thrilling thought because if it were up to me I will never make it. But since he is going to perfect me, he will get the job done. You may find this hard to believe but one day you will meet me and I will be perfect, and thank God because it will be his perfecting work. How he encourages us by grace and in a good hope. He is able not only to prevent me from falling – that is a miracle in itself – but he is able to present me faultless before his throne of grace.

147

The next thing God is going to do: he *protects*. He never promised us an easy time; life is a battle, the world is an alien and a hostile environment to anybody who wants to live with God. As soon as you try to live a better life you step out of your social group. A girl came to Spurgeon and said, "How much of the world should I give up now that I've become a Christian?" He said, "You don't need to bother about that – it's the world that will give you up." That is true provided you live a godly life. If you live a worldly life, then frankly the world won't give you up, but if you live a godly life your problem is to keep in touch with the world, not to separate from it.

We are in a hostile environment and we are so weak-willed. Somebody has defined will power as the ability to eat one salted peanut! We make resolutions every New Year; we decide we are going to make a clean start. Why does it all end in miserable failure? You read some of your old diaries and read the first ten days of January in those old diaries. Why? We are just so weak. Also we are facing a very strong enemy. Satan is a real, personal devil. If you have not yet discovered that, I wonder if you have discovered a real personal Lord. The devil is not in hell right now but in heavenly places. When you get through to those heavenly places you meet Jesus and the angels, you meet the devil too, and you begin to wrestle. Hand-to-hand wrestling – not with flesh and blood but with principalities and powers of darkness, spiritual hosts of wickedness.

What God does in that situation is to protect. It is his job. He protects me by doing two things: by strengthening me and weakening Satan. It is all here in this passage. He will protect you by girding you with strength and protecting you from the evil one. What more could you ask?

The fifth thing that God is going to do for us, and is doing for all those who believe, for all those whom he has chosen:

he is *directing* them. One of the great things about coming to church is that you get a sense of direction to your life. It is so easy to lose that in the humdrum, the busyness of getting on the train every morning, going to the office and coming back then just putting your feet up and trying to relax for the next day. It is like finding your way through a jungle. You are lost in the jungle and you do not know where you are going, you have just got to keep going. What do you do when lost in a jungle? You look around for a high tree and climb it. You look ahead and you will see your bearings. You see the mountain tops and you know where you are going. That is what we are doing on Sunday. We are leaving the office behind, climbing a tree, and looking ahead and saying, "Where are we going? What's the direction? What's it all about? What am I here for?"

The Lord directs us – to what? Love and loyalty. Every Sunday he lifts us up and invites us to look at these two mountain peaks – love and loyalty. The love of God and the constancy, the endurance, the perseverance, the loyalty of Jesus Christ. Now you will never find meaning in life until you find those two things. You see, some people think that when they've found love they have found life. That is not true, it is only half of the picture. That is why in a marriage service the couple is never asked "Do you love each other?" They are asked if they will be loyal to each other. It is assumed that they do love each other, and they are seeking to be directed in a Christian service to loyalty. You see, if it is just love then life may be a delight but it is a pretty poor thing by itself. If it's just loyalty then life becomes just a duty. What God wants to direct us towards is love and then loyalty – the kind of love that sticks, the kind of love that will go to the last ditch, the kind that Christ had in persevering, "Having loved his own he loved them to the end."

That is all God's work. He elects, connects, perfects,

protects and directs. Those five things can be regarded as God's hand, his fingers: you are in his hand and he will do those five things for you. So just go around his fingers when you count them on yours.

Now let us turn to the other side of things: human responsibility. The easiest thing in the world when you realise God's sovereignty is to say, "Well, there's nothing for me to do, it's all up to him; all right God, you can do it; carry on." That is a travesty of Christianity. The Christian faith puts as much emphasis on human responsibility as on divine sovereignty. They are so interwoven. The three things I am going to mention now just slot into the five things in the passage, and you move from the divine to the human and back again all the time. I have separated them out so that you may see them but it is really a sandwich. You put them back together.

Paul is writing to Christians so he does not include the responsibility of repenting and believing the gospel. That of course is the first human responsibility. If a human being goes to hell it is because he has not repented, and man must face that responsibility. God has not chosen to send him to hell – it is the man or woman's responsibility. But here are the responsibilities of Christians. First, we must *stay*. Second, we must *pray*. Third, we must *obey*. All of God's sovereignty without this human responsibility cannot bring about full salvation.

First: we *stay*. Now one difference between studying Christianity and anything else is this: you have a textbook two thousand years old that has not gone obsolete and never will, and has never been superseded by any later knowledge. That is intriguing. What would you think if you went to university to study mathematics and you were told, "Well now, the textbook was written two thousand years ago, there has never been any book since to beat it, and we are going to teach you this"? In any other area of human knowledge it would sound crazy. But in fact a Christian will never respond to God properly unless he goes back two thousand years for his basic knowledge.

Paul says: you must stay with the traditions we gave you. Now, I am not against tradition, I am just against the wrong ones. The church is so often a mixture of gothic architecture, Roman dress, Elizabethan language and Victorian music, and often stays with those traditions. What is my quarrel with those traditions? It is that they are not old enough, not that they are not young enough. It is the traditions that have crept in during the last two thousand years that are the difficulty. The traditions I want are the traditions of the apostles, and that is where we have got to stay. My quarrel is that it is subsequent traditions that have led us away from that. So I express nothing to you that was not said two thousand years ago. Isn't that strange? Yet, it is the most relevant and contemporary thing I could say. It is more up to date than tomorrow's newspaper. Isn't that marvellous? It must be divine inspiration.

So let's stay with traditions but not the wrong ones. Let's stay with the old ones, not the ones that are just a mere thousand years old, let us go to two thousand years old – that is where you get the real proper traditions. Those traditions came first of all in speech, but now of course they don't, they come now to us in written form. Thank God for those who wrote them down. The Bible is our traditional book. It will always be that way and we stay in this tradition. This tradition we must never let go. It is our responsibility to stay with it, and as long as I am free and able to breathe and to preach, I will tell people the old, old story of Jesus and his love. I will use up-to-date language and up-to-date illustrations, but I am a traditional man really.

The tragedy is that so often you will find an old-fashioned

church building, and old-fashioned music, and old fashioned everything else, and modern opinions in the pulpit. Isn't that a tragedy? I say that the traditions aren't going back far enough. I don't want to be modern in outlook, I want to be terribly old-fashioned. It is my responsibility to stay with it. What the apostles taught, I teach; what they spoke, I speak; what they wrote I must read and I must expound.

The second responsibility we have is to *pray*. It is so easy to say, "Look, if God predestines everything, why pray? If he decides everything, why ask him?" Don't let the devil argue you into that impossible logic – it is not true. If you realise what God is doing, you want to pray more and co-operate with him more. You want to be part of that, and so you pray more. Our responsibility is to pray particularly for two things and they are the two fundamental prayers of the Christian, our responsibility in seeing that God's work gets done. He is doing it, but it is our responsibility to pray that it may be done. First, we are to pray that the message may spread rapidly—may *run*. The Greek word used here was the fastest they could travel in those days. Of course, if you told a Greek man in those days that you could travel at thousands of miles an hour he would have laughed at you. The fastest they could go then was on a horse – that was real speed. Now the Word of God can go out so quickly. One of the things that thrills me, and for which I thank God, is the way the word I preach spreads throughout the whole world in the following months, or sometimes instantaneously. It used to be tapes and nowadays it is a variety of other media, enabling that prayer to be answered. Are you praying that the Word of God would get out as quickly as possible? It is a race against time. The population growth alone is a factor. There are countries closing to the gospel. The Wycliffe Bible translators published an account of their work under the title Two Thousand Tongues to Go – two thousand dialects and tongues to get the gospel into. Thank God for Christian media which in a split second can be used for the Word of God to speed around the world. Pray that the message may run rapidly.

One thing I would hate would be to be saying the same old thing to the same old people in the same old way year in and year out. The Word of God ought to spread rapidly, and every one of us ought to be praying that there would be new ways of getting it out quickly, spreading it more rapidly.

The second thing we need to pray for is that the messengers would be kept safe – not from physical harm but from human opposition. "For," as Paul says, and I translate it literally, "the faith is not for everyone." You can read into that what you like, but what it says to me is that those who do not have the faith cannot remain neutral, they become enemies of it. Have you ever noticed that? You are not in the position of a door-to-door salesman selling brushes – the people who refuse do not become your personal enemies. But when you spread the gospel, this is what happens. The people who refuse deep down subconsciously seem to know what they are doing and they become defensive and then aggressive. Pray for the messengers, because believe me, as we near the end of human history the opposition to the gospel is going to become terribly fierce and the messengers are going to be under severe attack. Pray!

Finally, we are to *obey*. I know it is an unmentionable word, but there it is: obey. "We obey." Now I don't know if you ever had this anxiety when you became a Christian, I know I did and I have had it since in relation to Christian service. I remember being interviewed by the Ministerial Recognition Committee of the Baptist Union and they said, "We've got a question to ask you. Now, we understand that in the Methodist ministry you preach two or three times a Quarter to the same people, therefore, only seven or eight times a year maybe to the same people, or maybe more often than that. Now in a Baptist church, you realise, you'll have to preach twice to the same people every Sunday – do you think you could keep it up?"

I must admit that there were moments when I thought, "How could I?" No public entertainer on television could keep it up. Writing their own material twice a week to the same audience? They need a team of scriptwriters. They have to have a series of shows and then go off. They couldn't keep it up – you ask them! I tell you this, the only way one can keep anything up in the Christian life is just this: we have confidence in the Lord—that's what Paul says here. We have confidence in the Lord; it is only our job to obey, and if I obey I can keep it up. That applies to the Christian life generally.

My cousin Tom Rees was at a boys' camp in his early days, and there was this little boy from the east end of London. At the end of the camp, Tom said, "Are you going to become a Christian before you go back home to London?"

"No, I'm not," he replied.

"Why? Don't you want to be?"

"Yes, I'd love to be."

"Well why don't you?"

This little lad then said to Tom, "Because I couldn't keep it up. If you knew my home, if you knew where I lived, and what it's like you would know I couldn't keep it up. So I'm not going to start."

Tom said, "Get hold of my wrists." The little lad got hold of his wrists, and Tom broke his hold. Then Tom said, "Now, put out your wrists." Tom was quite a big chap and he got hold of those little wrists and he said, "Now, you get out of mine."

He struggled and he pulled, but he couldn't! "Right," Tom said, "Now will you become a Christian? Because the

Lord will hold you."

How can we keep it up in an alien world? We never will. But Paul says, "I am confident in the Lord that you will obey and go on obeying; that you will achieve a consistency of life, that you will do what we have commanded." Because you see, you have only begun your job as a Christian evangelist when you have made a disciple and baptised them in the name of the Father, the Son, and the Holy Spirit. Jesus said, "Then go on to teach them to observe all that I have commanded you." How on earth will you achieve that? Paul says, "I'm confident in the Lord that you are obeying and that you will obey" – and that is your responsibility.

We have looked at divine sovereignty and human responsibility. There are two sides to a coin and you can never see both at once, but you cannot have a coin without them both. That is not an argument, it is an illustration of this fact. I see divine sovereignty on one side and I see human responsibility on the other side, and that is my wealth—both. How poor you become if you only see one of these two things. You can never unite them intellectually; you can never get them together logically. They belong to life, not logic. They belong to experience, not explanation. They belong to inspiration, not intellect. The human intellect has grappled with the problems of predestination and freewill and got no further forward, but I have got hold of the coin and I believe both. If you want any emphasis then I would put it where I have in this study: I gave you five points on divine sovereignty and three on human responsibility. It is not an equal thing, but they are both there and we must grasp both.

Alas, Christians involved in evangelism tend to stress too much the human will because their appeal is to a response to the gospel. They lose if they forget predestination as the base of their evangelism. In pastoral work and in church work we tend to overlook human responsibility and we love to dwell on the truths of divine sovereignty and what he does. But balanced Christianity – evangelism and pastoral work – is divine sovereignty and human responsibility as both sides of the same thing.

I cannot tie up all the questions, and I am terribly suspicious of someone who can, because invariably they fail to do justice to one of these two truths. But, I take them both humbly and say, "God, your thoughts are not my thoughts, and your ways are not my ways. But I praise you that it is all your work and you hold me responsible for my response."

10

Read 2 Thessalonians 3:6–end

A. DOCTRINE (6–10)
1. Lives – example
2. Lips – explanation

B. DISCIPLINE (11–15)
1. Conscience – exhortation
2. Community – excommunication

CONCLUSION
a. Greeting
b. Graphology
c. Grace

Reading between the lines, we find that one sin was infecting the fellowship at Thessalonica, and it was getting out of hand. It needed dealing with urgently. That sin was not lust, pride, greed, anger or envy, but it was one of those that have been listed among the seven deadly sins. It was sloth. That is not a sin we take too seriously. But the New Testament took it so seriously that Paul says if a man is lazy you should put him out of fellowship with you. That brings us right down to earth with a bump. So we need to think about work.

You see, sloth wastes money. It wastes time – not just your own, but other people's too, and that amounts to stealing. The old Jews used to have this proverb: "A man who doesn't teach his son a trade has taught him to steal." That is because he will always take more out of society than he puts into it. Therefore, what we are thinking about here is of very practical significance. More disturbing still was the reason behind the sloth. There are many natural reasons for sloth. Most of us like being lazy, wasting time doing nothing. But the reasons behind sloth here were not natural, they were spiritual reasons being done in the name of the Lord – which makes it ten times worse.

The kind of argument which was being given, and which sounded terribly spiritual, was this: the Lord is coming back so soon that time is short, we can't be bothered about getting an ordinary job or following an ordinary career; time is too short to work hard, we must all plunge into full-time service and redeem what bit of time is left. It is a false argument. If the Lord is coming back this week he wants to find us doing our daily work to his glory.

The classic story about that is of the freak storm that hit a small town in the southern states of America so that the sky went a kind of rusty red. There were strong gales and the whole place seemed to be shaking. In a certain courtroom a case was being tried before a judge, and in the courtroom the people panicked and said, "It's the second coming of the Lord." It was in the "Bible belt" of the middle part of America. The judge simply and calmly said, "Send for some candles. If the Lord is coming he must find us doing our work." Now, he had got the right end of the stick.

Because there is a tremendous sense in these days of things coming towards a climax, there is a widespread sense of the nearness of our Lord's coming, and of the fact that we could be the last generation of Christians on earth. All this has produced the same kind of thinking as it was producing in Thessalonica: a false deduction that therefore it is hardly worth training for a career, it is hardly worth getting a proper job. "Let's all get out on the streets; let's redeem the time." It sounds so spiritual but it is not scriptural. So Paul brings them down to earth with a bump. They are not to get so excited about the second coming but to go quietly off to work. That is how you should react to all this. So this is a very practical and rather sobering word for us.

Paul is, in effect, accusing some of playing truant, deserting their post, breaking ranks. He is pointing out that the church is like an army and Christians are soldiers. You have a duty, you have a post, and you must not desert it, and for practical purposes your post is your daily job. For too long now, Christians have thought of Christianity as something they do in their spare time. If that is how you think then you are wasting a third of your waking life if that is the proportion you spend at work – if that is not your job for the Lord. We want full time leisure so that we may be full-time Christians!

Let us go back to the scripture and see what it says. Bear in mind that this was written by a Hebrew man to Greek men and women. That may not sound a very startling statement but it is, because the Hebrew and the Greek attitudes to work were entirely opposite. Let me describe them briefly.

For the Greek, work was a necessary evil, to avoid if you possibly could. Their gods were not gods of work they were gods of leisure, and you become like the gods you worship. They worshipped gods who played around. You read Greek mythology and about the Greek deities. There is hardly one of them that does a day's work. They may do some spectacular feat now and again – like the labours of Hercules, and then he has finished. After some cleaning out of the stables, he is done. But the Greek gods and goddesses were not workers. Therefore, the Greeks – following the gods they worshipped, having created them I believe in their own image – did not want to work. If you could get a slave to do your work, fine. If you could get someone else to take over your job, and live a life of leisure so that you could follow interesting pursuits and hobbies, then you had achieved the purpose of life. So the aim of life was to cut the working hours down and down, and to increase the number of leisure hours that you had. Happy were you if you achieved that, and of course two-thirds of the people were slaves and did the work and the rest lived lives of leisure. They were thought to be the people who really lived. Does that sound strangely modern to you? Does that sound a bit related to our society?

The Hebrews thought very differently because the Hebrews worshipped a God who was a worker – and that is how the Bible begins. When Jesus, the Son, came on earth he said, "My Father works until now, and now I work." It is a sobering thought, which every Christian should remember, that the Son of God, sent to save the world, was only allowed to perform his full-time ministry of preaching for three years. For eighteen years the Father put him in a carpenter's shop and he worked with his hands. From this came a biblical outlook which saw that your daily work is the main purpose of your existence, the main channel of your fulfilling God's calling, your main offering of praise to him.

Therefore, your work was the big thing, not your leisure. It is intriguing that one of his commandments for the Jews did include the phrase "Six days shall you labour". We tend to think that commandment is all about the seventh, but it is not. Six days' labour. Work as hard as God does – that is what the Word of God said to the Jews. No five day or four day weeks there. You need rest, yes, but in order to be good workers like God, as God rested himself from his work of creation. That is the Hebrew doctrine of work.

There is another contrast between the Greek and the Hebrew. If the Greek had to work he would rather work with his head than his hands. To work with your hands was to be way down the social ladder, whereas to work with your head was to be at least one step up. It was at least a step away from hard labour, the drudgery of work. But to the Hebrew the true dignity of work lay with those who worked with their hands.

That is why Jesus, when he was given eighteen years' work, was given manual labour. That is why a Rabbi had to have a trade before he could be a Rabbi. Indeed, now more and more colleges for ministers and missionaries are insisting that a candidate has already qualified, already worked and made his mark in ordinary employment before considering full-time service. That is a very biblical approach. That is why Paul, though he had been to university and studied law, was in fact a tentmaker by trade. He worked with his hands like his Master before him.

Once again, do you see the contrast between the Greek wanting leisure rather than work and the Hebrews seeing purpose in work; the Greek seeing working with your head as somehow better than working with your hands, the Hebrew seeing working with your hands as better than working with your head? In these two, can you see that our society is far more deeply influenced by Greek than Hebrew thinking?

That is true not just in attitude to work but in almost every other sphere. It is one of the reasons why it is so difficult to preach the Bible and teach it in England today – because people have Greek values, Greek categories of thought, and you have to break through those to get through to the truth of the God of the Hebrews, because it is Hebrew thinking that is true to reality.

Paul is teaching that in relation to work you need two things: the right *doctrine* of work, and the right *discipline*. Our behaviour follows from our belief, and right doctrine produces the right sense of duty. So these two things are very much related.

Paul is saying: we gave you the right doctrine when we were with you – to your eyes through our example, and to your ears through our exposition. These were the two channels of teaching and they still are. The two great channels of teaching whereby doctrine reaches us are by lips and lives, and happy are those who receive such two-dimensional instruction.

But Paul says first of all: you saw that we worked hard. Now let me say a few things, which you have to think through and apply very carefully. First, it is the normal pattern for Christian life to earn the bread you eat, to be worth it to the people who support you. There will always be exceptions, and the early church was second to none in looking after the widows and orphans, those who did not have a breadwinner in the family and who could not earn their own bread. But the church was rightly stingy towards those who could work but didn't. In fact the church was very strict with spongers, loafers.

Missionaries would tell you that one of the problems in starting Christian work in a new country is the number of so called "rice Christians" that come round: people who will join the church for a bit of rice, who become sponges and who have to be supported by the mission station. One can see now that this is a short-sighted policy. When Paul opened up a new work as at Thessalonica, he not only preached the cross and the resurrection – he taught hard work.

Let us make it quite clear, secondly, that not only is it a normal position for a Christian to be supported by those whom he serves, to receive from them what he is worth, and to earn every bite that he eats, it is just as valid for a person to earn his bread by preaching or teaching the gospel as by baking bread. That is an important insight. Let us get it quite clear. 1 Corinthians 9 talks about the supported preacher as being in the same category as a labourer worthy of his hire. That statement goes back to our Lord himself, who sent out his labourers two by two and said: "If they want to give you bread, if they want to support you, receive it because a labourer is worthy of his hire." In other words: you are worth it, you are earning it from them, so take it. But it is in the category not of full-time Christian service as distinct from wage earning – you are simply earning your wages in a different way. That is an important insight. The Bible never draws a line between Christian service and any other service. All work is work if you are earning what you eat and if you are worth it to the people you are serving. In other words, normal employment is God's will for the Christian. It is only if he is in circumstances in which he cannot support himself that the church ought to undertake to carry him, but only in those circumstances.

Having said that, Paul says in 1 Corinthians 9 and he says here: "I had every right to be supported by you." But when Paul came to Thessalonica he had to do a bit of thinking. He had to realise he had come to a Greek audience with the gospel. He realised how they thought about work, and how, in that situation, if he did not actually work with his hands for his living but were to take support from them they would never accept his teaching. They would say, "Oh, he is only saying that because he was not prepared to work himself, and he thinks like we do." So, quite deliberately, he said, "I had the right to take my wages from you. I had the right to do it but I declined the right."

As somebody has said, "Whenever he declined the right he never forgot it." He always reminded people that he had the right to it. But in that Greek situation he saw that if they interpreted his life as sponging, as an easy one-day a week job, he would be misleading them and would not have the moral right to teach them. Every preacher of the gospel has honestly to ask himself if his taking wages for preaching the gospel is leading people who regard sponging and loafing or an easy job as the right thing in life. If people are getting that message then the minister just has to go out and get a job and kill that misunderstanding, and that is what Paul did.

So he said, "Our example was enough. Yet, we not only gave you an example, we spoke to you and gave you a rule." There are rules in the Christian life. It is a life of freedom to serve God and to be what God meant you to be. However it is not a life of lawlessness but of those who are under the law of liberty. Part of the law of liberty is the rule which Paul gave them. It is a stark rule: if a man will not work neither shall he eat.

I have only once in my life really refused to give someone a meal on the ground of this text. A young man in his late twenties or early thirties came and asked for a meal one day. He asked if we could give him lunch and said he had nothing to eat. Though I must admit humanly speaking I didn't find it easy to do, I had to say to that young man, "I'm sorry but the New Testament forbids me to give you lunch." He said, "Why?" I read him that verse. He was what is known as a "professional student". At the end of each course he managed to get on another one and convince a committee that he needed to do further research. He had done eight years – one course after another, about four or five courses. He had had thousands of pounds out of the taxpayers of this country, and seemed to have little sense of obligation to pay it back in any service to the community, and I am afraid I said that to him.

I praise God that the next time I saw him, which was about two years later, he had a job and he did have a meal with us. I don't know what has happened since, but it is a rule. It seems so hard, doesn't it? There ought to be much sympathy within the church, but no sentiment. I think the welfare state could learn something from this text. Yes, it is right to carry those who cannot get work, but it is criminal to make it more profitable for a man not to work than to go out and work with his hands and get something for his family. But here is the rule: if a man will not work then the church should not undertake his support. If he is not prepared to give value for money and could, then frankly the church is not interested. Tough? Yes. This applies whether the man is poor or rich. The Christian and the Communist, funnily enough, are agreed on this one thing: that a man who could work but does not work, whether he is rich or poor, is an offence to society. It does not matter whether you can afford not to work or not – if you can, the Bible says you should.

That is the doctrine, the teaching, and it has many ramifications. Let us move on to discipline. One of the difficulties is that those who are not busy in their own work usually make themselves busy in other people's. Have you noticed that? Paul has a lovely play on words which comes through in the translation: "They are not busy, they are busybodies" – that is a perfect translation of the Greek. The trouble is that if you are not busy doing your own job you fiddle around with other people's and tell them how to do it, or tell them they should take it easy as well. This attitude of sloth is terribly infectious. It spreads rapidly within Christian fellowship.

The trouble is that it unsettles others. If some young people manage to live without working and manage to go off and somehow survive somewhere, it soon unsettles the rest and they want to do it too. It spreads so quickly – this idea that you can actually live without having a regular job. You can get by, but it is a dangerously infectious disease. Paul deals with it now even more firmly.

Satan finds some mischief still for idle hands to do, and he finds mischief for idle mouths to do. There is a proverb in Arabia, which goes like this: "Satan tempts other men, but idle men tempt Satan." Now that is quite a statement! If you are not hard working yourself, you invariably go around telling others what they ought to do or ought not to do. It is true within churches, never mind daily work. The best cure for someone who is critical of things is to give them a job and get them into a job, and get them doing something for the Lord themselves. When you are busy doing something for yourself, you do not meddle with other people's jobs.

Now Paul appeals for discipline in two things: first to the person's conscience and then to the community; first to self-discipline within, and then to discipline from outside, in that order. So Paul now addresses those who are idle and says to them: "I appeal to you, I charge you, I command you, get back to your job." It is a strong word. In fact, he says, "Stop fussing, stop idling, and stop sponging." That is a very free translation, but I think it sums up what he is saying.

Take the first: work quietly. Have you ever noticed that the most efficient people are quiet in their work? You can always tell when someone is on top of his job because he does not fuss, he just quietly gets on with it. What a joy it is to see a worker who knows what he is doing. He will work quietly. Somebody has said in a comment on this which I think is delightful: "We are called to be the salt of the earth not the pepper, and we are called to shine in the world, but not to try and dazzle people." Work quietly, get on with the job, so that people maybe are not even aware that it is being done. That is the kind of efficiency that ought to be in Christian circles – not just in church work but in daily work.

So Paul is worried about the spread of this attitude: this general unsettling, this feeling of getting fed up with your job, of wanting to be out of it, of feeling hemmed in by being tied down to one job. My father is someone who worked all his working life in one room. He started in it at the beginning of his career; he finished in it at the end. He started as a reader in the university, then became a lecturer, then he became finally Professor, but he kept the room. When he retired, they gave him his room to go on using in the university. He was stuck to that desk for forty years. Nowadays we get restless after we have been two or three years in a place. We want to pull the roots up. It is part of the general malaise of our society. It is part of the feeling of restlessness that if we stay too long in one place we are going to miss an experience in another – we have to keep on the move. Paul says: never get tired of doing what is right. Don't get unsettled, don't get fed up, don't get itchy feet, don't get restless. Get on with the job; stay with it, don't get weary with it, just go on doing it. It is very sound and practical advice, but how much it is needed in our world.

Now supposing the appeal to the person's conscience does not work. Supposing he does not respond; supposing he says, "No, I'm not going to settle down to work. I just don't feel I can. I'm going to sit around until the Lord guides me to something new." That is a favourite statement. Look, you should not be thinking of something new unless, first, you are perfectly satisfied with what you are doing, and doing it well; and unless, second, you are prepared to stay in that until the Lord really makes it clear you should be doing something else. Just to drop everything and wait I don't think is scriptural. Whatever your hand finds to do, do it with all your might. Remain in the calling in which he called you. These are the emphases of the New Testament.

But supposing the person does not listen; supposing his conscience does not respond? Then Paul says that the church must act; the rest must do two things. I am putting them starkly because this will shatter you. He says: "First, blacklist the man who will not work, and second, send him to Coventry." Now this is the Bible we are reading, not a trade union manual. The Bible tells us to blacklist those who will not go to work. "Make a note of them," says Paul, "Mark them." That is strong language.

"Don't associate with them; withdraw from them." This is the way that any society brings pressure to bear on one of its members. This is the way that you communicate to others how you feel about what they are doing. Paul is saying let the church do this – if a man is not working hard, let them just withdraw. Don't have fellowship with that man. On the other hand, and here comes the balancing factor, though in doing this and blacklisting and sending him to Coventry, you are showing that you do not condone his attitude to work, you must nevertheless not condemn him or write him off. Remember all the time that he is a brother, not an enemy. It is getting the balance right in Christian discipline that is so difficult. Churches so easily go to one extreme or the other. We either do not have any discipline at all and do not withdraw fellowship from any, or become so strict that you make everybody an enemy and cut them off for good. But the balance is there.

It happens in every family. What parent has not at some stage said to their child: "Now go up to your bedroom, and when you can behave properly and relate to the rest of the family properly, you can come down." Have you not said that? The church is a family as well as an army. The church sometimes needs to say to someone: "Go away by yourself until you can behave properly as a member of the family." The real test as to whether the church is treating the person as a brother or an enemy is this: when they have put it right and they have come back, what is your attitude then? If you still regard them as a brother then your arms are flung out to receive them in love. If you have treated them as an enemy and written them off, you are embarrassed to have them back. That is the discipline of the community: tough language, family language; the responsibility of the whole church.

Strange, isn't it, that a man's secular work is of concern to the church? You may say, "But it's of no business to the fellowship. I earn my business up in London, or I do this, or I do that." It is the business of the church because the church is to reflect the character of the Lord. God is a worker, so the church should reflect that character and should be seen to be good workers who stay in their jobs and who keep their jobs, and who do a good day's work for a good day's pay, and who are labourers worthy of their hire.

Finally we come to the last three verses. What a lovely message: now may the Lord of peace himself give you peace at all times and in every way. I guess that covers most of it. I am so sorry we have not got a better word in English than "peace". I know it is a lovely word which has got a nice ring about it, but it does not get across the meaning of the word Paul used – *shalom*, which signifies total harmony. It means physical harmony so that your body is working in harmony, and therefore it means health; it means social harmony with your relatives, your friends, even with your enemies. That is a lovely thing and still included in the word *shalom*. It means harmony with the Lord so that you and he walk together as friends. It includes all that and so much more – harmony in every sphere of life. May your work go well, may you be in harmony with your job, harmony with your boss. May you live in a world of harmony in which there will be different notes, different varieties of experience, yet all fitting together. No discord there, but a harmony of life so that all the experiences make up a whole symphony of praise and thanksgiving. It is all in this little word *shalom*. May the God of shalom give you shalom at all times and in every way – the harmony that comes not through running away from problems, not through changing your job, but by the Lord's presence right there. For the peace is related to his presence. Paul immediately goes on: "The Lord be with you all" – you cannot have shalom without him. He is the God of shalom and you will never have peace without the God of peace; they belong together.

Then Paul remembers that people have written letters in his name and said dreadful things, and misled young Christians by forging his signature. So with that scrawly handwriting of his, due to his poor eyesight, he takes the pen from his secretary, having dictated most of the letter, and he says, "Now, here's my authentic writing in my own hand" as he peers at the parchment – a little personal touch.

Then he finishes with the secret of it all: "The grace of the Lord Jesus Christ be with all of you." It is the same blessing that he gave at the end of 1 Thessalonians with the addition of one word which he put in especially here. At the end of 1 Thessalonians he said, "The grace of the Lord Jesus Christ be with you." Here he says, "With you all" – including those loafers, including those busybodies, including those you may have to discipline – the grace of the Lord Jesus Christ be with you all. May not one of you miss out on that grace.

Books by David Pawson available from **www.davidpawsonbooks.com**

A Commentary on the Gospel of **Mark**
A Commentary on the Gospel of **John**
A Commentary on **Acts**
A Commentary on **Romans**
A Commentary on **Galatians**
A Commentary on **1 & 2 Thessalonians**
A Commentary on **Hebrews**
A Commentary on **James**
A Commentary on **The Letters of John**
A Commentary on **Jude**
A Commentary on the Book of **Revelation**
By God, I Will (The Biblical Covenants)
Angels
Christianity Explained
Come with me through **Isaiah**
Defending Christian Zionism
Explaining the Resurrection
Explaining the Second Coming
Explaining Water Baptism
Is John 3:16 the Gospel?
Israel in the New Testament
Jesus Baptises in One Holy Spirit
Jesus: The Seven Wonders of HIStory
Leadership is Male
Living in Hope
Not as Bad as the Truth (autobiography)
Once Saved, Always Saved?
Practising the Principles of Prayer
Remarriage is Adultery Unless....
The Challenge of Islam to Christians
The Character of God
The God and the Gospel of Righteousness
The Lord's Prayer
The Maker's Instructions (Ten Commandments)
The Normal Christian Birth
The Road to Hell
Unlocking the Bible
What the Bible says about the Holy Spirit
When Jesus Returns
Where has the Body been for 2000 years?
Where is Jesus Now?
Why Does God Allow Natural Disasters?
Word and Spirit Together

Unlocking the Bible
is also available in DVD format from **www.davidpawson.com**

Lightning Source UK Ltd.
Milton Keynes UK
UKOW06f2307220415

250126UK00001B/6/P

9 781909 886735